HOME
HYDROPONICS

HOME
HYDROPONICS
...and how to do it!

REVISED AND UPDATED

by Lem Jones
with
Paul and Cay Beardsley

CROWN PUBLISHERS, INC.
NEW YORK

Copyright © 1977 by Lem Jones

Published by Crown Publishers, Inc., 201 East 50th Street New York, New York 10022

CROWN is a trademark of Crown Publishers, Inc.

Manufactured in the United States of America

Library of Congress Cataloging-in-Publication Data

Jones, J.L. (John Lemuel), 1907–
    Home hydroponics...and how to do it!

    Includes bibliographical references.
    1. Hydroponics. I. Beardsley, Paul. II. Beardsley.
Cay. III. Title
SB126.5.J66 1990   631.5'85   90-1823

ISBN 0-517-53760-5

10 9 8 7 6

This book is dedicated to my family, who have made so many sacrifices the past fifteen years, thereby making it possible for me to continue in this field, and in memory of my beloved son John L. Jones, III.

Contents

Acknowledgments

In looking back over nearly fifteen years of work in hydroponics, I can reach only one conclusion: what little success I have enjoyed is because of the many fine people who have not only given me advice and encouragement but have so generously allowed me to share in their vast accumulation of knowledge.

I owe much to Clayton Murr of Junction, Texas, whose encouragement and generosity were responsible for my entry into the field of hydroponics. Also my brother, Jack Jones, whose help was invaluable in the early years, as was that of the late Charles Barrett of Harper, Texas. Leading a long list of others are Dr. Paul Chatelier and his wife, Mary, St. Petersburg, Florida; Dr. Edward Saub, Anaheim, California; J. D. Evans, Florida College, Temple Terrace, Florida; Jay S. Fichtner, John and Barbara Groo, David Linder, and William Schenk, all of Dallas, Texas; and C. C. Qualls, Albuquerque, New Mexico.

Dr. John E. Larsen of Texas A&M University, with whom I have often argued the merits of hydroponics versus soil in greenhouse vegetable culture, is another who has been of much help to me over the years. A suggestion by Dr. Larsen started me on my first attempt to build a Quonset type greenhouse. That first prototype evolved into what is today the most widely used and copied building and hydroponic system in the world.

I am indebted to Dr. Merle H. Jensen of the Environmental Research Laboratory, University of Arizona, Tucson, Arizona, and Dr. Raymond Sheldrake of Cornell University, Ithaca, New York, who have given generously of their time and knowledge in solving many problems.

Although visits with Dr. S. H. Wittwer, Director of the Agricultural Experiment Station, Michigan State University, Lansing, Michigan, have been too infrequent and short, they have aided me in many areas of vegetable production.

During the time spent in constructing a 100-unit hydroponic complex near Byron, Georgia, the help of Mary Francis Neal was invaluable.

Over the past eight years there are many who have given me help and advice for which I will be forever grateful. Those to whom I owe special acknowledgment are: Dr. Donald Black, Roy Peck, Dick Myers, Lewis Gregory, Bob Yount, Wally Shores, Harry Heflin, Oscar Ackleson, A. E. Bard, Gene Symcox, Bill Duree, Jack McFalls, Terry Chidekel, Carol and Bob Bremer, Lola Mack, Caulene Mason, Al Sterner, Dick Clancy, Rick Wood, and Lupe Anaya.

Malcolm L. Lentz and Jack Latham (president and vice-president, respectively) of Hydroculture, Inc. have graciously allowed the use of many of their fine photos. Credit for some pictures and line illustrations must also go to Paul R. Beardsley.

Throughout these past fifteen years I have visited with growers all over the United States and several foreign countries. Every one of them, through their comments and observations, have added to my knowledge. Among those whose advice and friendship have meant much are Edythe and Ray Knox, Houston, Texas; Jane and Louis Huckert, Bakersfield, California; David Lambert, Seattle, Washington, Kay and Jerry Covey, San Angelo, Texas; Jacqueline Rosseau, Peoria, Arizona; Repps B. Guitar, Jr., Abilene,

Texas; Bob and Melba Ladd, Mena, Arkansas; and Khalid Nahouli and Abdul Rahman Kriedieh of Beirut, Lebanon. To all of them plus the hundreds of other growers I have known, many thanks.

Without the help, advice, and encouragement of Cay and Paul Beardsley, I could never have written this book.

All sources of information, seeds, trade names, and other materials listed in this book are intended as aids to the reader and to not imply approval of any particular source or brand name to the exclusion of others that may be equally suitable.

HOME
HYDROPONICS

The Past, Present, and Future

The science of growing plants without soil has been known and used for more than 100 years. The word *hydroponics*, however, is comparatively new. Dr. W. E. Gericke, who contributed a great deal to the art as it is practiced today, is usually given credit for coining the word, which translated from Greek, means working water. True hydroponic culture is generally a means of growing plants in a nutrient solution using no soil or other rooting medium, although today almost all of the many different methods of growing plants without soil employ various types of inert materials for a rooting medium, such as gravel, hadite, perlite, vermiculite, pumice, sand, and others.

In delving into the history of hydroponics, the famous hanging gardens of Babylon—one of the seven wonders of the ancient world—was probably one of the first attempts to grow plants hydroponically. The floating gardens of the Aztecs of Mexico and those of the Chinese, as described by Marco Polo in his famous journal, were, in a sense, also hydroponic. The ancient Egyptians practiced the art in some form, as they described growing plants in water in hieroglyphic records dating to several hundred years B.C.

In 1699 an Englishman, Woodward, proved that plants could be grown in water by dissolving soil in it, and he concluded that soil itself was not necessary. Certain elements needed by the plants (most of them unknown) were released when the soil was dissolved and thus were taken up by the plants.

De Saussre theorized in 1804 that plants were made up of elements derived from water, soil, and air. Another Frenchman, Boussingault, proved this theory correct by growing plants in sand and feeding them with various chemical solutions. In 1856 Salm-Horsmar developed techniques using sand and other inert media, and between 1860 and 1865, Sachs and Knop developed techniques that enabled them to grow plants in a nutrient solution. Their systems are still used by researchers today.

The work of Dr. Gericke in the 1920s and 1930s in California, however, is generally considered the basis for nearly all forms of hydroponics. During the time Dr. Gericke was working, he received a great deal of publicity about his method of growing vegetables. This brought on a considerable boom in hydroponics. Variations of Dr. Gericke's methods are still in use, but many would-be hydroponic growers encountered problems with the Gericke system because it required a great deal of technical knowledge and ingenuity to build. Gericke's system consisted of a series of troughs or basins over which he stretched a fine wire mesh. This in turn was covered by a mulch of straw or other material. The plants were placed on this mesh, with the roots extending downward into a nutrient solution in the basin.

One of the main difficulties with this method was keeping a sufficient supply of oxygen in the nutrient solution. The plants would exhaust the oxygen rapidly, taking it up through the roots, and for this reason it was imperative that a continuous supply of fresh oxygen be introduced into the solution through some method of aeration. Another problem was supporting the plants so that the growing tips of the roots were held in the solution properly.

During the 1940s at Purdue University, Robert B. and Alice P. Withrow developed another hydroponic method. Their process was called Nutriculture, and coupled with the need during World War II to grow fresh vegetables for troops stationed in areas not suitable for conventional agriculture, it gave hydroponics a new impetus. Nutriculture differed from Dr. Gericke's method in that gravel was used as a rooting medium.

One of the first of several large hydroponic farms was built on Ascension Island in the South Atlantic, using techniques based largely on the work of the Withrows. Ascension was used as a rest and fuel stop by the United States Air Force, and the island was completely barren. Since it was necessary to keep a large force there to service planes, all food had to be flown or shipped in. There was a critical need for fresh vegetables, and for this reason the first of many such hydroponic installations established by our armed forces was built there. The plants were grown in a gravel medium with the solution pumped into the gravel on a preset cycle.

Techniques developed on Ascension were used in later installations on various islands in the Pacific such as Iwo Jima and Okinawa. Later, during the occupation, it became necessary to use hydroponics in Japan because of the method of fertilizing soil used by the Japanese. It had been their practice for many years to use "night soil," containing human excreta as a fertilizer. The soil was highly contaminated with various types of bacteria and amoeba, and although the Japanese were immune to these organisms, the occupying troops were not. The largest hydroponic installations up to that time were built in Japan using the gravel culture method.

After World War II a number of commercial installations were built in the United States. The majority of these were located in Florida. Most were out of doors and subject to the rigors of the weather. Poor construction techniques and operating practices caused many of them to be unsuccessful and production inconsistent.

One of the many problems encountered by the early hydroponics pioneers was caused by the concrete used for the growing beds. Lime and other elements leached into the solution. In addition most metal was also affected by the various elements in the solution. In many of these early gardens, galvanized and iron pipe were used. Not only did they corrode very quickly, but elements harmful or toxic to the plants were released into the nutrient solution.

Nevertheless, interest in hydroponic culture continued for several reasons. First, no soil was needed, and a large plant population could be grown in a very small area. Second, when fed properly, optimum production could be attained. With most vegetables, growth was accelerated and, as a rule, the quality was better than that of soil-grown vegetables. Produce grown hydroponically had much longer shelf life or keeping qualities.

Many of the oil and mining companies built large gardens at some of their installations in different parts of the world where conventional farming methods were not feasible. Some were in desert areas with little or no rainfall or subsurface waters, and others were on islands, such as those in the Caribbean, with little or no soil suitable for vegetable production.

In addition to the large commercial systems built between 1945 and the 1960s, much work was done on small units for use in apartments, homes, and back yards for growing both flowers and vegetables. Many of these were not a complete success because of a number of factors: poor rooting media, the use of unsuitable materials, particularly in constructing the troughs used as growing beds, and crude environmental control. Even with the lack of success in many of these ventures, however, hydroponic growers the world over were convinced that their problems could be solved. There was also a growing conviction in the minds of many that the perfection of this method of growing food was absolutely essential in light of declining food production and the worldwide population explosion.

In addition to the work being done to develop hydroponic systems for the production of vegetables, however, between 1930 and 1960 similar work was being conducted to develop a system to produce livestock and poultry feed. Researchers had found that cereal grains could be grown very rapidly in this manner. Using grains such as barley, they proved that 5 pounds of seed could be converted into 35 pounds of lush green feed in 7 days. When used as a supplement to normal rations, this green feed was extremely beneficial for all types of animals and birds. In lactating animals milk flow was increased. In the feed lots, better conversion rates and gains were achieved at less cost per pound of gain. In breeding stock the potency of males and conception in females increased dramatically. Poultry also benefited in many ways. Egg production increased while cannibalism, a constant problem for poultrymen, ceased.

Here again, however, in developing a system that would produce consistently, a number of problems arose. The early systems had little or no environmental control, and with no control of temperatures or humidity, there was constant fluctuation in the growth rate. Mold and fungi in the grasses were an ever-present problem. The use of thoroughly clean seed grain with a high germination ratio was found to be absolutely essential if a good growth rate was to be achieved.

Nevertheless, in the face of these and other obstacles, a few dedicated researchers continued to work to perfect a system that could produce this nutritious feed continuously. With the development of new techniques, equipment, and materials, units became available that were virtually trouble free. Many of these are in use today on ranches, farms, and in zoos all over the world.

If there is one single factor that could be credited with making the hydroponics industry the success it is today, that factor is plastics. As mentioned earlier, one of the most pressing problems encountered everywhere was the constant leaching of detrimental elements into the solution from concrete, rooting media, and other materials. With the advent of fiberglass and such plastics as the different types of vinyl, polyethelene film, and the many kinds of plastic pipe, this problem was virtually eliminated. In the better-producing systems being built in the world today plastics are used throughout, and other than bronze valves, there is absolutely no metal. Even the pumps are epoxy coated. Using these types of materials, along with an inert material as a rooting medium, the grower is well on his way to success.

Another important breakthrough was the development of a completely balanced plant food. Work in this area is still continuing, but there are many ready-made formulas available. Most of them are good, but very few, if any, will work consistently without the use of various additives at different stages in the crop. There are also many formulas available that can be mixed by anyone, but the average grower is far better off using one of the many commercial formulas.

In addition to the progress made through the use of plastics and the steady increase in production because of improved nutrient mixes, another factor of tremendous importance to the future of the industry was the development of better hardware for control of the environment in greenhouses. Initially, nearly all of the early greenhouses were steam heated, and the cost of this equipment virtually barred the small grower from entering this field. With the development of forced-draft heaters that used oil or gas, however, it became possible to build much smaller units, and the advent of LP gas, such as butane and propane, made possible the location of greenhouses in almost any area.

Constant improvements in these heating systems, particularly the introduction of high-velocity fans and the convection tube method of circulating warm air throughout a building, gave the grower better temperature control in the greenhouse. For commercial operations in larger greenhouses, however, a boiler system using steam or hot water remained the most economical. It gave the grower wide latitude in the choice of fuel. There has also been continuous improvement in techniques and equipment for cooling any size greenhouse.

In addition to better environmental control, the use of new materials such as polyethelene, poly-vinyl films, and translucent fiberglass panels introduced completely new methods of greenhouse construction. They gave the builder a wide choice of material for covering any size unit and also made possible many new shapes, sizes, and configurations. Some of these materials will last only one season; others are guaranteed for 20 years against clouding that causes light loss and against shattering from hail. I have seen fiberglass-covered buildings hit by heavy hail; despite damage to the cover, there was little or no damage to the crop. Had a light film or glass been used, however, both the crop and cover would have been completely lost. The films are good for temporary or semitemporary cover. Many of these materials also give light diffusion that is beneficial to most plants.

The combination of environmental control and improved hydroponic systems has largely been responsible for the growth of the industry over the past fifteen years, and there can be no question that hydroponics will play a big part in feeding the world in the future. As an example of the need for hydroponics, in 1950 there was a total of 3.7 million acres of land under cultivation in the United States.

At that time the population in the United States was 150,718,000. In 1970 the total acreage in cultivation had dropped to 3.2 million and the population had grown to 204,000,000. In the next twenty years, it is estimated that the population of the United States will grow to 278,570,000 —an increase of 79,000,000 people. It is hard to project how many more acres will be lost to production during this time.[1]

The Salt River Valley, which surrounds Phoenix, Arizona, illustrates what happens when the population explodes in an area. The growth pattern of the Salt River Valley is characteristic of many areas not only in the United States, but the world over. The first settlers who came into this area were looking for good land and water, both of which existed in the Salt River Valley. After World War II, the excellent climate caused a massive population boom.

In 1950, within the boundaries of the Salt River Project, there were 239,802 acres, of which 225,152 acres were assessed as agricultural lands. Between 1950 and 1960, these agricultural lands decreased by 37,795 acres. There was a further decrease of 35,411 acres between 1960 and 1970. Between 1971 and 1973, there was an additional loss of 19,172 acres. In 23 years a total of 92,378 acres have been taken out of crop production forever.[2]

The pace at which this fine land is disappearing from production is constantly accelerating. At the current rate, by 1990 there will be little, if any, cultivated land left within the present boundaries of the Salt River Project.

Traveling over the United States, one can see the same pattern being followed elsewhere. Another classic example is Southern California, particularly the Los Angeles area with its tremendous urban sprawl.

1. United States Department of Agriculture and United States Department of Commerce.
2. Mr. Reid W. Teeples, Associate General Manager—Water, Salt River Project, Phoenix, Arizona.

With hydroponics there is no need for soil, and only about one twenty-fifth as much water is needed as in conventional farming. The hydroponic growers of the future will be using the roof tops of warehouses and other large buildings on which to install commercial systems. Here there is ample space. All that is needed in addition to this space is electricity, fuel, and water. Systems built in this manner will have the added advantage of being at, or near, the market place, eliminating the need for long-distance transportation of produce such as we have today. Because the environment within the hydroponic installations can be controlled, these systems can produce vegetables year-round in almost any climate.

There is no question that we already have the technology to build systems such as I have just described. There will, however, be other systems built by or for the home owner that will take up very little space. Some of these will be small enough to be installed in the kitchen or other parts of the home. They will produce an abundant supply of many types of foods, particularly lettuce, strawberries, and similar crops. There are already workable units of this type available now.

In other areas of the world, such as the Middle East, there is little land suitable for farming. Because of the development of the oil industry and the subsequent flow of wealth, the building of large hydroponic farms to feed the exploding populations in these nations is inevitable. If there is any one industry in the world today whose time has come, it is hydroponics.

Another area in which hydroponics promises to play an important role in the future is growing seedlings for reforestation, orchards, and ornamental shrubbery. In a report published in 1966, researchers at the University of Wisconsin stated that seedlings of white cedar, blue and white spruce, red pine, and others were grown in a controlled environment. Using a hydroponic system with controlled feedings of a nutrient solution, the results of growth in one year were three to four times as great as in year-old nursery-grown seedlings. The extension of the growing season in this northern area, through the use of hydroponics and more concentrated use of space, made it possible to grow five to ten times as many plants in a given area. Some plantings of pine were 18 years old at the time this report was published and were said to be growing vigorously.[3]

But there continue to be problems that hamper the growth and development of hydroponics as a whole. One problem is the negative attitude of people in many of our colleges, universities, and government agencies, which has ranged from complete disinterest to open hostility. This attitude partly results from their own failure to achieve crop yields matching those of many hydroponic growers. Fortunately, in some of our schools there are people who not only have open minds but who have also given generously of their time and talents to help growers with their problems.

Another problem that has developed in the past few years is the ever-increasing cost of energy for heating. In many areas the high cost of fuel has caused a number of installations that were operating at a profit to suddenly plunge deeply into the red, and some operators have been forced to shut down entirely in the colder months. Since this is the time of year when vegetables are at or near peak prices, these increased fuel costs have had a disastrous effect on the industry.

One bright spot in this picture is the development of solar heating systems. Much research has and is being done in this field, and there are many ready-built systems available on the market today. Also available are a number of publications with detailed plans on how to build one's own

3. *American Nursery Man*, 1966.

solar energy system. An excellent book on this subject is *How To Build A Solar Heater* by Ted Lucas (see suppliers list). There will, of course, be many new developments in this field over the next few years, and solar energy may eventually solve the dilemma for hydroponic growers.

The biggest danger to the growth and development of hydroponics has been the influx of "instant experts" over the past 10 years. The success of many growers using properly designed equipment has attracted these self-styled authorities in ever-growing numbers. Making extravagant claims, they have sold many shabby, poorly made copies of workable units with the assurance that this was the easy road to riches. Many of these fly-by-night promotions have been short lived but, sadly, others continue to flourish.

The cost to the would-be commercial grower for a properly designed hydroponic system, housed in a manner that provides good environmental control, can run into thousands of dollars. For this reason he should check very closely on the qualifications of the seller. He should require proof of claims regarding production and profit capability, back-up service after the sale, research facilities, and past records of the manufacturing company.

If a person is willing to work and apply himself, plants can be grown hydroponically by a complete novice with no past experience at growing crops. Hydroponics can also be profitable on a commercial scale if the grower devotes the time and attention required for any successful business. Hydroponics is a fascinating method of growing plants and can give the hobbyist or serious grower many hours of pleasure.

Simple Systems—
Equipment—
Greenhouse

Many people today sprout beans and grains such as mung beans and alfalfa at home, and almost everyone has grown a sweet potato in a jar of water. This is nothing more than hydroponics and is the simplest form of the science in use today.

Simple Systems: Indoor and Outdoor

Figure 1 shows a simple hydroponic system that uses an inert medium. The materials needed are easily obtainable, and the system is very simple to construct. You need a two-gallon plastic pail and a plastic dishpan, and you must construct a small frame. Many people have built variations of this system. A styrofoam ice box also makes an excellent container for the growing medium.

This is a simple hydroponic system easy enough for a youngster to build and operate. Build the frame with a 6-inch square hole. It must be high enough for a pail to fit underneath. The cork or stopper should be removed from below. An oval plastic pan is preferable for holding the roofing medium.

15

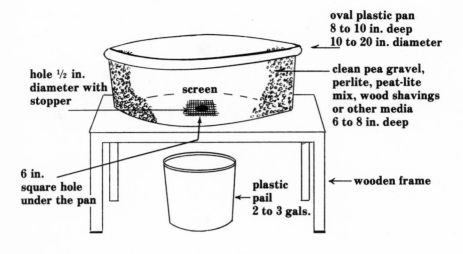

FIGURE 1.
Simple Hydroponic System

Place a plastic screen over the hole to keep the rooting medium in the pan. Fill the pan with the medium, and mix the plant food with water, pouring the solution gently into the medium.

Use enough of the solution to bring the solution level to within ½ inch of the top of the medium (top ½ inch should always be dry). Plant seeds or set plants in the medium just as you would in soil. Let the solution drain into the pail. Feed the plants in this manner two to three times daily, letting solution stand in the medium 10 to 15 minutes each time. Check the pH (see p. 73) each morning, using vinegar or aspirin to bring it to the correct level. Make up fresh solution weekly.

As your plants and evaporation deplete the solution, make up the lost amount of fluid at the same ratio of plant food to water as the original solution. Give the plants as much sunlight as possible. If used inside, a small "Gro-Lux" light will promote good growth where adequate sunlight is not available. Follow the instructions in chapters 3 and 4 relating to care and selection of seeds.

Some of the vegetables and flowers that do well in this system are tomatoes, green onions, lettuce, peppers, radishes, tulips, roses, coleus, amaryllis, ivy, and many others. Any plant grown in the soil can be grown in this manner, although some are more adaptable than others to hydroponic or gravel culture.

Important: *Before mixing the plant food with water, you should adjust the pH of the raw water. Most city water has a pH of approximately 8.0. The correct pH for growing most plants hydroponically is approximately 6.2. Two aspirin tablets dissolved per gallon of water will usually bring the pH very near the correct level. White vinegar can also be used. Add 1 tablespoon per gallon of water; test and adjust if necessary. This should always be done before adding the plant food to the water. Test the pH again after the nutrient is added to the water. (See chapter 3 for instructions on pH testing and control.)*

For the hobbyist or beginner, simple container systems can be purchased but you must remember that almost all plants need a certain amount of sunlight. If sunlight is not available there are "gro-lights" on the market that will give good results. In the winter months, I have had best results by placing the units in front of a window that had a southern or southeastern exposure and then supplementing available light with the "Gro-Lux" or similar lights, which give off a wide band spectrum (see suppliers list).

Another system that is simple to construct and operate is shown in figure 2. The materials used to construct it, as shown in figures 2 and 3, are a terrarium 12 inches in diameter (this one made by Phillips Products), a Beckett pump model #100 Nugget, a small spray nozzle such as the type that can be inserted in a small bottle and used to dampen clothes for ironing, and a 30-minute constant-cycle timer.

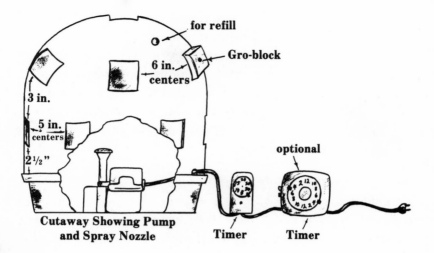

for refill

Gro-block

6 in.
centers

3 in.

5 in.
centers

2½"

**Cutaway Showing Pump
and Spray Nozzle**

optional

Timer

Timer

**FIGURE 2.
Terrarium Converted to Hydroponic Spray System
(not drawn to scale)**

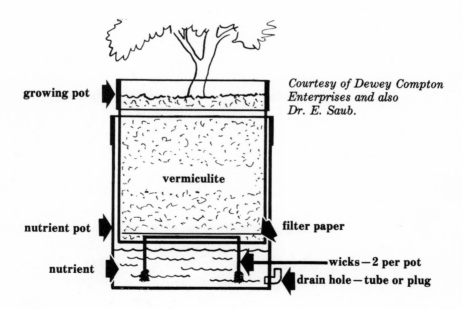

growing pot

*Courtesy of Dewey Compton
Enterprises and also
Dr. E. Saub.*

vermiculite

nutrient pot

filter paper

nutrient

wicks — 2 per pot

drain hole — tube or plug

**FIGURE 3.
The Wick System**

18

If these items cannot be found locally, see the suppliers list. (Terrariums—Mellingers; Pumps—Beckett Pump Company; Timer—W. W. Granger; Nozzle—local hardware store.)

Using an electric soldering iron, modified as described for figure 6, cut holes in the terrarium as shown in figure 2. The small, round hole is used to refill the system as needed.

The dome of the terrarium should be painted to make it opaque. I prefer a white paint or enamel such as that used for painting appliances.

For this particular system, I start the seedlings in BR8 Blocks (see suppliers list). When the seedlings are two to three weeks old, the blocks are inserted in the square holes. Any excess fiber that may be loose should be trimmed off to lessen the possibility that it will fall into the solution and clog up the pump intake.

The blocks should be moist so that by compressing them they may be easily forced into the holes. About a third of the block should protrude through to the outside and be tilted slightly upward. When the block is in place, press on the top and bottom at the same time to cause it to expand tightly against the sides of the hole.

The receptacle that forms the bottom section of the terrarium should then be filled with the nutrient solution, made from any good hydroponic nutrient (see suppliers list). This solution should be replaced every 10 days. The dome may be lifted off the bottom receptacle by inserting a finger in the small refill hole and lifting straight up. As the plants begin to develop, care must be taken not to disturb or harm the roots.

When the unit has been planted as described, adjust the timer so that the pump will be actuated for 30 seconds out of each 30-minute cycle. It will be necessary to add small amounts of water every two or three days to replace that taken up by the plants and ensure an adequate supply in the unit at all times.

If you have a pH test kit, maintain the solution at or near 6.5 for lettuce. One or two aspirin tablets per gallon of water should be sufficient to buffer the raw water and bring it to the correct pH.

The spray nozzle should be checked from time to time to make sure all of the holes are open and that the pump is throwing a good spray pattern.

When the unit is all planted and ready to be put in operation, it should be placed where it can receive an adequate amount of sunlight, if at all possible. If you put it near a window, it will be necessary to rotate the unit daily. It is best to place these units in front of a window with a southern exposure and then suspend a small Gro-Lux light slightly above the unit on the opposite side from the window.

By planting two or three blocks for replacement seedlings each week, one of these small units will furnish a constant supply of lettuce the year round. I have produced excellent lettuce using the following varieties: Ostinata, Great Lakes, Salad Bowl, Bibb, and Chesibb.

There are similar ready-built systems on the market (see page 52). This type of system can also be used to grow other vegetables such as small tomatoes and strawberries, but adjustments will have to be made for the moisture needs of the different varieties of vegetables. If it is to be used for strawberries, it will be necessary to use a second timer. This timer should be a 24-hour, day-night type that can be adjusted to completely deactivate the system so that the strawberry plants are fed for a short time each day. One point to remember about strawberries, however, is that it is very easy to over water them. Whatever variety of plant you are growing, you can, by trial and error, adjust the system to promote good growth and production.

Still another very simple hydroponic system that almost anyone can build employs a wick system, as shown in figure 3. For those who do not wish to build their own, these are also available ready-built (see suppliers list).

Two 5-gallon plastic pails will make a very satisfactory system, but they must be opaque. In one of the pails, drill four holes in the bottom. Any absorbent material may be used as a wick. One half-inch cotton rope will be satisfactory. Thread the rope through the holes as shown. Be sure to unravel at least one inch or more from the ends to make them more absorbent. Place a piece of filter paper, such as a good quality paper towel, over the wick inside the pail to cover the bottom.

When the wick and filter paper are in place, fill the container with finely ground vermiculite #3 or #4 to within 2 inches of the top. Run water through the vermiculite until it is well soaked. Mix 4 to 6 quarts of nutrient solution made up from a good formula into the other container. Then place the pail containing the vermiculite inside the one holding the nutrient solution. The wicks extending down will draw the nutrient solution up into the vermiculite.

The system is now ready for planting with either seeds or transplants. Check your solution every two or three days at the beginning to be sure there is an ample supply in the bottom of the container. After a few days, you will learn by experience how much water should be added between solution changes to keep the solution at the proper level. When the system is first started, it should be checked daily to be sure enough moisture is being drawn up to germinate the seeds or feed the transplants.

The solution should be changed every 10 days. A new solution may be poured directly into the vermiculite, but it is better to lift out the pail containing the plants and pour the new solution directly into the bottom container.

Be sure there is enough dry vermiculite at the top of the container at all times to prevent the growth of algae.

One of the many ready-built systems available is the Tube-o-Ponic, as shown in figure 4. In this system the nutrient solution is stored in the circular tank that encloses the bottom of the tube. A small pump lifts the solution to

*Courtesy of Dewey Compton
Enterprises and also
Dr. E. Saub.*

FIGURE 4.
Tube-o-Ponic System

the top of the tube, where a breaker type of nozzle allows a constant drip to fall on the roots of the plants, which are held in place in the openings on the sides of the tube.

Outdoors a level area 12 x 20 feet is large enough to provide a sufficient quantity of vegetables for the average family. By building a two-bed, one-sump system in this space, you will have approximately 80 square feet of growing area. These bed systems should be installed in a shade-free area. If there is some shade, be sure the beds are placed so they are not shaded during the morning hours.

These outdoor bed and sump systems can be constructed as shown in figures 7, 8, 9 and 10. The construction of the sump and beds is the same whether used outdoors or in a greenhouse. Climate will determine the length of time these outdoor beds can be operated, but in any case, it is advisable to construct a simple protective overhead cover of either vinyl film or translucent fiberglass. This will not only provide support necessary to string up tomatoes, cucumbers, melons, and other plants, but will also provide shade for the system. Even more important, it will protect the crop from heavy rains. In areas where there are strong prevailing winds, it may also be necessary to erect a wind break.

Two Unique Hydroponic Systems

An alternate and somewhat unique hydroponic bed system involves the use of spray nozzles, as shown in figure 5. In this system there is no need for any inert medium. This system works well with almost all plants, particularly tomatoes, strawberries, and lettuce. Pumping cycles are controlled by timers, as shown. The styrofoam cover should cover the entire bed.

This system may be used in a greenhouse or outside (if weather permits). The bed is constructed as shown in figures 7 and 8. One bed end has holes for fill and drain lines as shown. Use ¾-inch plastic pipe with plastic spray nozzles.

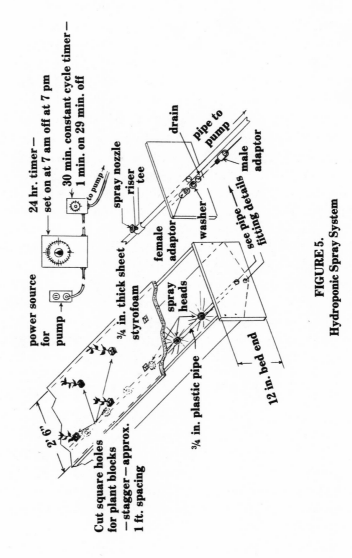

FIGURE 5.
Hydroponic Spray System

Nozzles must be arranged to give good coverage of the root system and should be placed approximately 2 feet apart. A plastic lawn hose soaker may be used in place of the plastic pipe and nozzles. This also must be arranged for good coverage of the root system.

This system requires two timers—a constant-cycle timer set 1 minute on and 29 minutes off to control the spray nozzles and a 24-hour timer set to go on at 7:00 A.M. and off at 7:00 P.M. to control the constant-cycle timer. Pump cycles may be shortened or lengthened according to plant needs and temperatures. The approximate pump size for a growing bed 2½ x 16 feet should be 250 GPH at a 3-foot head to give adequate pressure.

Use ¾-inch styrofoam to make the bed cover. Fasten or weight the cover. Carefully cut square holes (to fit the planting blocks) approximately 1 foot apart, staggered.

Construct the sump as shown in figure 9. It should hold at least 40 gallons of water. For this size bed, a sump measuring 2 x 2 x 2 feet that holds approximately 60 gallons will suffice. A large plastic garbage container will make an adequate sump for a small one-bed system.

This system is particularly good for tomatoes, cucumbers, and lettuce. If you are growing tomatoes and cucumbers, you must erect a frame or wire over the bed on which to attach a string to tie up the plants (see page 95).

Another unique hydroponic growing system involves the use of large tubes, or troughs, as shown in figure 6. Solution-laden water is pumped up to water the planting blocks.

This system can be installed in a greenhouse or, climate and weather permitting, outside. In this system three to five growing pipes may be used (figure 6 shows three pipes for illustrative purposes).

Build a frame of 2 x 4s. Mount metal brackets to hold 4-inch growing pipes. All piping and fittings must be plastic. Use thin-wall plastic piping 4 inches in diameter for the growing pipes. Cut square holes in the growing pipes for

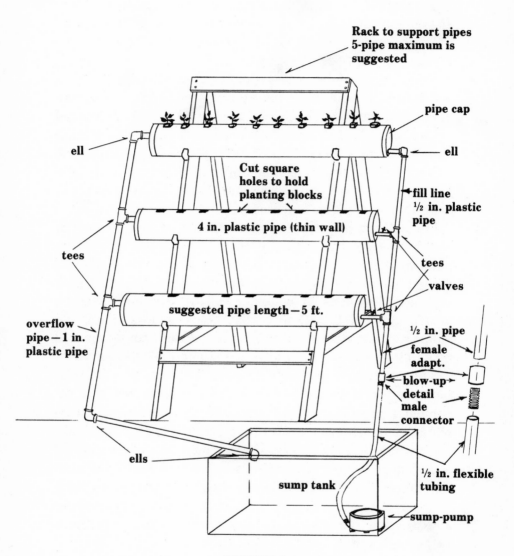

Rack to support pipes
5-pipe maximum is
suggested

pipe cap

ell

ell

Cut square
holes to hold
planting blocks

fill line
½ in. plastic
pipe

4 in. plastic pipe (thin wall)

tees

tees

valves

suggested pipe length — 5 ft.

overflow
pipe — 1 in.
plastic pipe

½ in. pipe

female
adapt.

blow-up
detail
male
connector

ells

½ in. flexible
tubing

sump tank

sump-pump

FIGURE 6.
Hydroponic Tube and Rack System for
Lettuce, Strawberries, Green Plants,
and Small Flowers

the planting blocks using an electric soldering iron with the tip filed down to a thin knife edge. Holes should be spaced 6 inches apart. They should measure approximately 1¼ to 1-5/8 inches square, depending on the size of the growing block. Use ½-inch pipe for the fill line and 1-inch pipe for the overflow line, all ells and tees sized to fit.

Glue a pipe cap to each end of the growing pipes. Cut five pieces each of ½-inch and 1-inch pipe, 4 inches long (10 pieces total). Use them to connect tees and ells into the ends of the growing pipes. Carefully drill holes to size. Drill a hole ¼ inch from the *bottom* edge of each cap on the *fill-line* side. This will cause the water to fill the growing pipes from the bottom. Drill a hole ½ inch from the *top* edge of each cap on the overflow-pipe side. This will allow the water to reach the growing blocks and root systems of the plants before flowing out the overflow pipe. Insert 4-inch pipe lengths into cap approximately 1 inch (do *not* glue until *all* pipes and fittings have been cut and fitted together).

A sump tank with a 24-gallon capacity is adequate for this system. It can be constructed as shown in figure 9. Approximate size should be 2 x 2 feet square by 1 foot high, which will hold 30 gallons of water. A lid should cover the sump. A porcelain livestock watering tank can be used. Do *not* use a metal tank. The top of the sump must sit below the bottom edge of the lowest growing pipe. It can be above or below ground level.

If it is above ground level, it would be convenient to have a plug near the bottom of one end to drain the sump. Also, a hose can be attached to the flexible tubing to transfer the solution to other growing beds or a lawn. Be sure to neutralize the pH before re-using the solution.

A submersible, recirculating pump rated at 300 GPH should be used for this size rack and sump.

Place growing pipes on the rack. Cut all other pipes to measure. Fit all pipes into tees and ells *before* gluing any of the pipes and fittings.

Use the same timer layout as in figure 5. A constant cycle timer should activate the pump for approximately 1 minute out of every 30 minutes. It may be adjusted to ensure complete filling and circulation of the nutrient solution through the pipes. A 24-hour timer should be set to turn the system on at 7:00 A.M. and off at 7:00 P.M.

See figure 1 for determining the pH level. Follow instructions in chapters 3 and 4 on plant nutrition and care, selecting seeds, and growing seedlings. When the seedlings are ready to be planted, fill the sump, test the water, and neutralize it if necessary. Add the nutrient and retest the water. Carefully inset any roots that may extend out of the growing blocks into the precut squares, and place the blocks into the holes. Each block should extend out of the hole approximately 1/4 to 5/8 inch. Set the timers and start the system. When the timer goes off, all remaining solution will drain back into the sump through the fill line.

This is an excellent system for growing strawberries, lettuce, patio tomatoes, and many other plant varieties.

Controlled Environmental Greenhouses

For the grower who would like to set up a system with a controlled environment for use year round, the best small greenhouses that can be built at home are the gothic arch types such as the one designed at the University of Kentucky. Complete plans for building this type of greenhouse can be found at the end of this chapter.

These gothic-shaped greenhouses are adaptable to almost any location and should be positioned so that prevailing winds strike the rear of the structures. They can be covered with either PVC film or translucent fiberglass panels. With either type of covering, it is very easy to line the interior of this particular type of greenhouse with film. When fastened in place properly, this lining creates an insulating air space. This will not only reduce heat loss and heating costs by at least 30 percent but will also help eliminate condensation on the covering inside the greenhouse.

One practice that I particularly recommend is to spray the covering on the inside of the greenhouse with "Sun Clear" (see suppliers list). This substance will hydrolize the surface, and condensation will not remain on the film or panels as it forms but will drain off immediately. Heavy condensation on the cover of the greenhouse can reduce greatly the amount of sunlight reaching the plants, but water dripping on the plants from condensation can create other problems. This is especially true in the colder months, and during that period of the year it is of utmost importance for the plants to receive as much sunlight as possible.

It has been my experience that a unit measuring 12 x 20 feet, with a minimum center height of 9 feet is ideal for the backyard grower. Smaller buildings are very hard to cool properly and do not allow enough growing space for the variety of plants and flowers most growers desire.

The plans and specifications in this book are calculated for a greenhouse 12 x 20 x 9 feet.

Ground Preparation

After the site has been leveled, a sandy loam or a soil and gravel mix should be used to form a pad 6 inches high. This pad should extend at least 2 feet outward from the walls of the building. If a cement slab is poured, it should be set on top of this pad. This will lessen or eliminate any chance of flooding in the building. Always keep weeds and grass from growing near the building, as these are excellent breeding grounds for insects.

Sump-Tank Placement

There are two methods of handling the placement of the sump-tank in relation to the beds. The most common method is to sink the sump-tank into the ground so that the top of the sump-tank is approximately level with the bottom of the beds. This means the beds will be positioned at floor level. If you wish to have raised beds, set the sump-tank at floor level and raise the beds proportionately.

Growing Beds

In constructing the growing beds, it is absolutely essential that there be no leaks whatsoever. A very small hole will cause the loss of a great deal of solution. Since the normal operating procedure is to refill the tank to the proper operating level with fresh water each day, too much leakage will cause a decided dilution of the nutrient, and very shortly the plant will begin to exhibit signs of starvation.

In a 12 x 20 x 9-foot greenhouse, the beds should be 16 feet long. This allows space for the heaters and good air circulation. The beds should be approximately 30 inches wide. This width will allow space for two or three rows of plants. A wider bed will not allow enough sunlight or proper air circulation. Beds should be approximately 8 to 10 inches deep.

One type of bed is shown in figure 7. Build a side frame of 2 x 6-inch redwood or cedar to desired length as shown. Set it in place and stake it. Level it across and slope it lengthwise toward the sump tank ½ inch for each 10 feet of length.

Excavate the bed to shape as shown. The excavation should be 2 inches larger overall to allow for sand fill. Pour sand in the excavation, dampen, shape, and pack to configuration. Take vinyl film 10 mils or heavier and lay it in place, fitting it to the contour of the bed. Tack or staple it to the top of the 2 x 6-inch side frame.

Lay the perforated pipe; then set the bulkhead (½-inch plywood) in place and nail it. Fit bed ends (¼-inch plywood) in place and nail to 2 x 6 ends. Fit vinyl film inside bed end

30

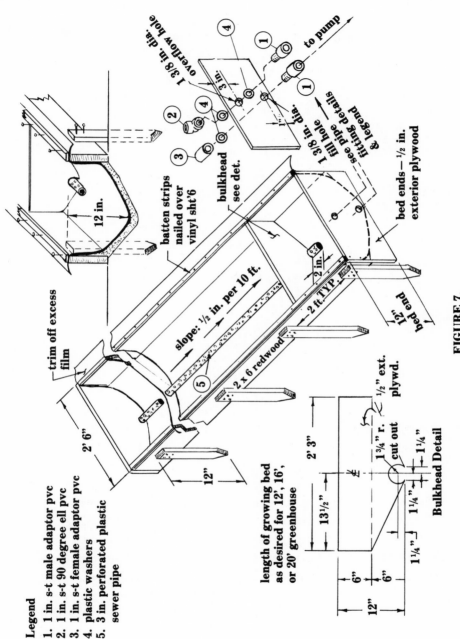

Legend
1. 1 in. s-t male adaptor pvc
2. 1 in. s-t 90 degree ell pvc
3. 1 in. s-t female adaptor pvc
4. plastic washers
5. 3 in. perforated plastic sewer pipe

length of growing bed as desired for 12', 16', or 20' greenhouse

1 3/8 in. dia. overflow hole.

to pump

3 in.

1 3/8 in. dia. fill hole

see pipe details fitting legend

1"

bed ends — 1/2 in. exterior plywood

bulkhead see det.

batten strips nailed over vinyl sht'6

trim off excess film

slope: 1/2 in. per 10 ft.

2 x 6 redwood

2 ft. TYP.

2 in.

12 in.

2' 6"

12"

12"
bed end

Bulkhead Detail

1/2" ext. plywd.

1 3/4" r. cut out

2' 3"

13 1/2"

1 1/4"

1 1/4"

1 1/4"

6"

6"

12"

FIGURE 7.
Film-Lined Bed

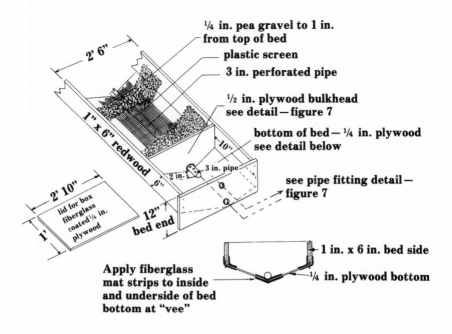

FIGURE 8.
Fiberglass-Coated Bed

as snugly as possible, and cut holes in film for a tight fit over threaded end of male adapter. Use care, and do not oversize. Fit adapters through holes in the bed ends, then through hole in the film. Slip a plastic washer over the threads of the adapter; oil threads and washer; screw on the female coupling. Couplings must be tight in order to compress the washer against the film to avoid leaking.

Cover perforated pipe with a strip of plastic screen (see figure 8). This is necessary to keep the pipe from clogging with gravel or other media. If desired, solid plastic pipe may be used by drilling four rows of 3/16-inch holes lengthwise. Space the holes 4 inches apart. This will eliminate the screen. Pour in gravel, and fill the bed to within 1 inch of the top. Nail lath over the film along the edge of the frame.

Trim off excess film. The solution will pump from the sump into the end box (between the bed and bulkhead), then into the perforated pipe to fill the bed. It drains back into the sump when the pump shuts off.

Another type of bed is shown in figure 8. The sides of the bed are constructed of 1 x 6-inch dressed lumber or redwood. The ends, lid, and bulkhead are made of ½-inch plywood. Use ¼-inch plywood for the bed bottom.

Cut lumber to size, nail it together, and tack plywood bottom pieces at "V" using small wire nails.

When fiberglass is dry, set the beds in place. Sink the beds so that 4 inches of the sides are above the ground level. Slope the beds toward the sump ½ inch for every 10 feet of length. Pack soil firmly around and under the bed.

Install perforated pipe, screen, gravel, and fittings as shown in figure 7. For beds up to 16 feet long, use 1-inch pipe and fittings; on longer lengths use 1½-inch pipes and fittings.

Fiberglass mat, resin, catalyst (MEK), rollers, brushes, acetone for cleaning tools, and other supplies can be purchased from Cook Paint Stores, boat companies, and other local sources. Care must be used in mixing the catalyst and resin. Use of too much catalyst will cause the mix to heat and cure too fast. It may also be heated to the point of spontaneous combustion. Do *not* store these substances together or near flammable materials.

Sump-Tank Size

When calculating the size of the sump-tank you will need, you must take into consideration several factors. One of these is the minimum gallonage necessary for good plant growth in a hydroponic system. The tank must be large enough to hold sufficient nutrient solution to completely irrigate the growing beds. It is best to have a tank large enough so that at least 20 percent of the solution is left in the tank when the solution reaches the top of the beds. By having this reserve, you will always have an adequate supply of solution. Each time the pump (or pumps) operates and irrigates the growing beds, some of the solution will be lost from uptake by the plants and through evaporation, which points up the necessity for the reserve.

To determine the size of the sump-tank needed, you must find the cubic footage of the bed. Calculate as follows: multiply the width, 2 feet, 6 inches—by the length, 16 feet—by the depth (gravel depth), 8 inches. In this case it would be 26 cubic feet. This, multiplied by 7½ (the approximate number of gallons per cubic foot), would give you 195 gallons. The space taken up by the gravel is two-thirds of the volume. You then divide 195 gallons by 3, giving you 65 gallons. This would be the *absolute minimum* needed to irrigate one bed. You must *double* this figure for *two* beds—approximately 130 gallons. To be on the safe side and have a reserve, allow another 20 gallons. You would, therefore, need a sump-tank capable of holding approximately 150 gallons. The approximate size sump-tank needed to hold this gallonage would be 2 feet wide, by 3½ feet long, by 3 feet deep.

Construction details for sump and sump-pipe fitting layout are shown in figures 9 and 10.

Use ½-inch plywood to construct the sump. Use plastic-coated nails if possible. All fittings and pipe should be plastic. The sump is buried in the ground.

The "pump well" is formed by cutting a 1-foot square hole in the bottom of the sump. Rim the hole on the *bottom* side with 2 x 2s. Attach a 1-foot square plywood cover to form the bottom of the pump well.

Fiberglass the sump inside and outside, following the instructions in figure 8. Reinforce all corners with fiberglass matting strips.

Cut and fit all piping before gluing (see figure 10 for details).

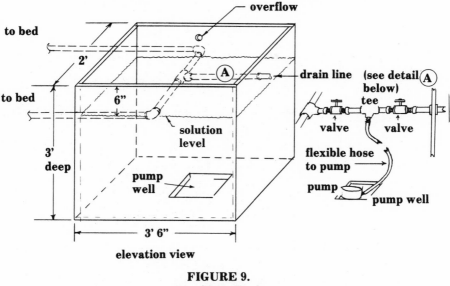

to bed

overflow

2'

to bed

6"

solution
level

3'
deep

pump
well

(A)

drain line (see detail (A) below)

tee

valve   valve

flexible hose
to pump

pump

pump well

3' 6"

elevation view

FIGURE 9.
The Sump-Tank

Two control valves are needed. One controls the entry of the water into the beds; the other is opened to drain the sump.

Sink the sump into the ground deep enough so that the piping will extend straight into the growing beds.

One factor that many growers have difficulty understanding is that the normal solution loss through leakage, plant uptake, or evaporation creates two problems in maintaining a proper nutrient balance. It will cause the dilution of some of the elements in the solution and at the same time cause higher concentration, or buildup, of other elements, such as the nitrates.

If the grower is a competent chemist and has the necessary equipment for testing the solution, adding a small amount of plant food each day, he can maintain his solution at the proper ranges. Since a very small percentage of hydroponic growers have the necessary equipment or know-how to do this, however, the average grower will

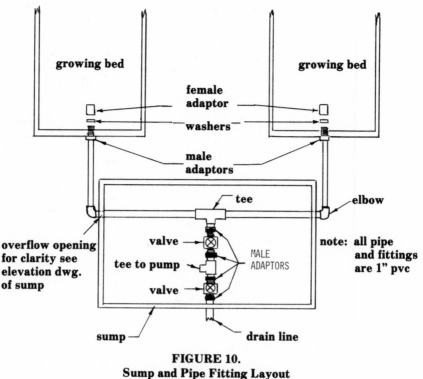

FIGURE 10.
Sump and Pipe Fitting Layout
(top view)

achieve better success by dumping the solution once every eight days and refilling the tank with a new supply. By operating his system in this manner, the various elements needed for good plant growth can be kept in balance and within the correct ranges.

Many knowledgeable hydroponic operators who are interested primarily in tomato production base their calculations on the number of plants in the growing bed. Based on the correct spacing of plants in a bed of the dimensions in figures 7 and 8, the operator would have 32 tomato plants. Using a rule of 2 gallons of solution per plant will give the approximate same 65-gallon minimum tank capacity for each bed.

Sump-Tank Pumps

Each bed is serviced by a submersible pump. All pumps are rated by the manufacturers in gallons-per-hour at different heads or lift. For the dimensions of a growing bed and sump-tank as shown above, you would need a pump with a capability of producing approximately 5 gallons per minute or 300 gallons per hour. In 15 minutes one pump would pump 75 gallons of solution into one growing bed. A slightly larger pump that would pump 75 gallons of solution into the growing beds in 10 minutes is even better. One extremely important factor in good hydroponic procedure is to be able to fill the growing bed from the tank as rapidly as possible. The solution should drain back into the tank at about the same rate.

Sump-Pumps and Timing

Long pumping cycles and slow drain-back are two of the reasons many growers have poor production. Properly sized equipment that will fill the bed and return the solution to the tank in less than 30 minutes will give the best results. A complete cycle in 20 minutes would be even better. If the solution stands in the bed very long, most plants will begin to suffer from the lack of oxygen, much as a person will who remains under water too long. The plants will simply drown from lack of fresh oxygen to the roots.

I once received a call from a new grower whose tomatoes had almost reached the picking stage when the plants suddenly began to die. In questioning him as to the possible cause, I found that he had lengthened the pumping cycle and had been overwatering the plants. They had started to wilt, and the more they wilted the more solution he pumped to them. Finally, in desperation, he pumped his growing beds full and left the solution standing in the beds overnight as well as a good part of the next day. A couple of days later, with this continued excess pumping, every plant in his greenhouse was dead or dying. He had simply drowned them.

You should usually set the pump timer so that the pumped solution level is approximately 1½ inches below the top of the gravel. The timer can be mounted on a control board at the front of the greenhouse (see plans at the end of this chapter). If a bed is constructed with an overflow (1½ inches below the top of the gravel), the pumping cycle can be set for a little longer period of time, letting the solution circulate from the tank into the growing bed and back through the overflow system. This action will aerate the solution well by adding oxygen and keeping the solution stirred.

Sump-Tank Lid

It is important to have a good lid covering the sump-tank. The lid should be kept in place at all times. Failure to keep a lid on the tank will cause algae to form in the solution and on the walls of the tank. It will also cause a change in the pH as well as a loss of iron in the solution. Having an open tank is definitely a hazard as well and could easily result in serious injury.

If a rim or lip is built around the upper side of the sump lid, this area can be used for starting seedlings. A small hole for drainage should be in the corner. The lid should have handles as shown in figure 11 so that it can be moved easily

Use 3/8-inch plywood. Nail frame of 1 x 2-inch lumber as shown for seedling tray. Cover with fiberglass. Use rubber bumpers fastened with screws to the underside of the lid to hold it in place.

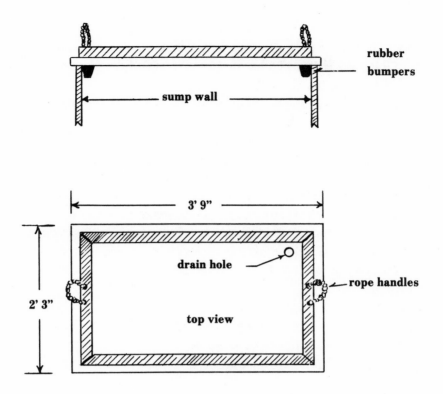

FIGURE 11.
Sump Tank Lid Cover and Seedling Tray

Heating

To determine the size of the heating equipment you will need, you must consider what it will take to maintain the proper temperatures inside regardless of outdoor temperatures. Then you should determine the type and placement of heaters that will fit your particular needs.

Heating requirements for a greenhouse are based on the following (Example: 12 x 20 x 9-foot greenhouse).

- Total area of exposed covering.
- Minimum outdoor temperatures, usually based on average lows. (To be on the safe side, you should take into account the record low in your area.)
- Temperatures to be maintained in the greenhouse.

Different amounts of heat are lost through glass, film, and fiberglass. A factor of 1.2 BTUs per square foot of exposed area of film or fiberglass is considered safe.

If the greenhouse is heated by LP or natural gas, the BTU output of heaters needed is figured as follows:

—Figure the total exposed surface: square footage of side walls, roof, and ends. Example: 816 square feet x 1.2= 980 BTUs for exposed square footage.

- Outside minimum temperature, 0°F.
- Desired inside temperature, 60°F.
- Differential then would be 60°F.
- 60 x 980=58,800 BTUs.

If electric heaters are to be used, the size of the heaters needed may be calculated at 23 watts per 100 square feet of exposed covering. Using the same total as above (816 square feet) adjusted to 850 square feet for additional safety, 23 x 8.5=196 watts, and 196 watts x 1.2=235 electric watts.

These formulas are for single-wall structures. If double-wall structures are used, with either type of heating the output may be reduced by 25 percent.

Two heaters, each giving half the desired output, are preferred. Heaters should be placed at or near ground level and positioned as shown in figure 12 to give better circulation. Gas heaters must be vented and some provisions made for introducing fresh air while the heaters are operating. This can be done by placing a small air vent, 2 x 6 inches, in the wall behind each heater. If this is not done, gas damage to plants will occur.

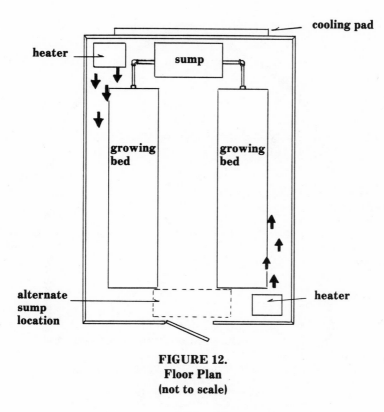

FIGURE 12.
Floor Plan
(not to scale)

Cooling

In a small greenhouse of this type, it is necessary to equip the building with a cooling system and a method of complete air exchange. There are two principal methods of cooling one may use. The first of these involves "pulling" the air through the unit. A cooling pad system is installed at the rear of the unit as shown in figure 13.

The water circulation system and pad must be kept open and clean at all times so that the cooling pad is kept moist over the entire area. A factor known as static pressure occurs when the fans are operating and the air is being drawn through the cooling pad. Static pressure is created when water flows over the surface of the pad and restricts the flow of air through the pad. The denser the pad, the higher the static pressure. The static pressure also rises

41

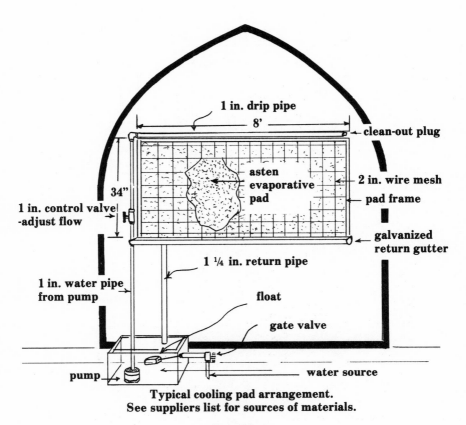

1 in. drip pipe

8'

clean-out plug

asten
evaporative
pad

2 in. wire mesh

pad frame

34"

**1 in. control valve
-adjust flow**

galvanized
return gutter

1 ¼ in. return pipe

**1 in. water pipe
from pump**

float

gate valve

pump

water source

Typical cooling pad arrangement.
See suppliers list for sources of materials.

FIGURE 13.
Interior — Rear Wall

when water is circulated on the pad, as this creates more resistance to the air flow.

The air flow will tend to increase through any dry spots on the pad or through any holes or cracks where there is no resistance. A surprisingly large amount of air will enter through such cracks or holes instead of through the wet pad, thus reducing the cooling effect. For this reason much care should be given to the construction of the pad and of the building itself. When the cooling fans are running, all of the air entering the building must flow through the wet pad.

On the front of the unit, two exhaust fans are installed as shown in figure 14. To determine fan sizes and cooling pad

42

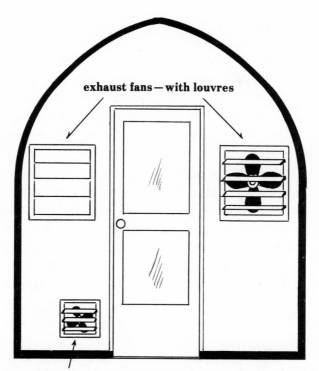

exhaust fans—with louvres

small humidity fan pulls heavy, damp air out at floor level

FIGURE 14.
Exterior — Front Wall

dimensions, multiply the length of the building by the width: 12 x 20 feet=240 square feet of floor space. This, multiplied by 10, equals slightly more than the cubic feet contained in the greenhouse and allows for resistance from static pressure since 10 x 240=2400, this 2400 cubic feet of air is the amount that should be pulled through the greenhouse per minute.

Since all exhaust fans are rated by CFM, it is an easy matter to select the correct size. Two fans, pulling approximately 1200 CFM each, are preferred over one rated at approximately 2400 CFM.

The cooling pad should contain one square foot of pad surface for each 150 CFM, so two fans pulling 1200 CFM each would require 16 square feet of pad surface, a pad approximately 2 x 8 feet long, in areas up to 1000 feet above sea level. As the elevation rises, fan sizes should be increased 5 percent per thousand feet of altitude gained. For example, at 5000 feet above sea level, fan CFM would be increased from 1250 CFM to 1600 CFM, and pad surface would be increased by slightly over 3 square feet. For a small greenhouse, it is far better to oversize rather than undersize the fans.

The pump used, for circulating water over the cooling pad should pump ½ gallon of water per minute per linear foot of cooling pad. A pad 8 feet long would require 4 gallons per minute. The pump would be rated at 180 GPH at a 6-foot head (the height at which the water comes out of the discharge pipe of the pump). The drip line pipe should be equipped with a control valve as shown in figure 13 so you can adjust the flow of water over pad.

To control the exhaust fans, thermostats are used. In the smaller units, a single-stage thermostat that operates both fans at the same time will be satisfactory. This same thermostat should activate the cooling pad pump at the rear of the building so that the pump will begin circulating water over the cooling pad when the exhaust fans come on.

You may, however, wish to use a two-stage thermostat that will turn on one fan at one setting and as the temperature begins to rise, activate the other fan. If a two-stage system is used, the first fan to begin operating will pull only dry air through the building. As the temperature rises, the pump circulating water over the cooling pad will be turned on in conjunction with the second fan. This two-stage system gives somewhat better control over the air movement and cooling than the single-stage setup. Thermostat settings for heating and cooling are given later in this chapter.

One important factor for you to remember is that often in the cooler months bright sunshine will raise the temperature within the building very rapidly, even though outdoor temperatures may still be low and in some areas near the

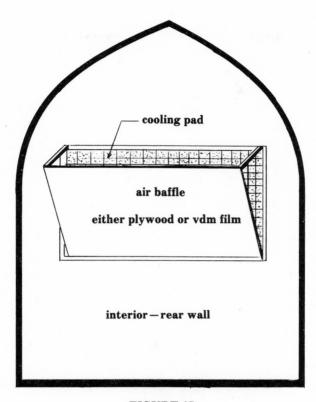

FIGURE 15.
Air Baffle

freezing mark. When this condition occurs, the fans will be activated and cold air drawn into the greenhouse. This cold air, striking the plants in the rear of the building, will have a very negative effect on them and can cause serious injury. You should arrange a baffle as shown in figure 15 to divert the air over and away from the plants.

In colder climates many operators shut down the cooling system in the cold months. If this is done, some method must be used to introduce a small supply of fresh air into the building. I recommend leaving a small portion of the cooling pad area uncovered. A gas heater will very rapidly exhaust the oxygen within the building, and this will have an extremely adverse effect on the plants. A small (2 x 6-inch) louvered vent behind the heater is essential. Where the building is closed up tightly with no introduction of fresh air, CO_2 levels will become virtually nonexistent, again affecting the plants.

Another piece of equipment of vital importance to a controlled environment is a small exhaust fan installed as shown in figure 14. This fan is to be used for humidity control and should be installed near floor level. It should be sized to exhaust one-fourth of the total cubic feet of air in the building per minute. For example, with 2000 cubic feet, the fan should be rated at 500 CFM. This fan can be controlled by a humidistat. When the temperature drops to where the exhaust fans for cooling cut off, humidity in the building will immediately begin to rise. The heaters coming on will counteract this somewhat if properly vented, but transpiration from the plants and irrigation cycles will further contribute to this increase of humidity. As will be discussed in later chapters, different plants produce and develop at various humidity levels. Excessive humidity will make the greenhouse ripe for an outbreak of fungi and in tomatoes will create problems such as lack of pollination and fruit set, all of which will contribute to poor production. Another method used by some growers to actuate the humidity exhaust fan is a timing device similar to the timers used to control the pumps. If a timer is used, the trippers are set to actuate the fan 5 to 10 minutes out of each hour. It should be wired so that it operates only when the cooling fans are off.

The second cooling method involves "pushing" air through the unit. Evaporative coolers (I recommend two) should be positioned at the rear of the unit as shown in top photo. To estimate the size of the coolers needed for the house in the example, use the same formula for sizing exhaust fans. The coolers will have recirculating pumps controlled by humidistats. It would be best to consult the manufacturer of the coolers to ascertain proper sizing on these pumps. On the front of the unit there should be two

Placement of evaporative coolers and louvered exhaust ports.

louvered exhaust ports (see photo p. 47). These should measure approximately 12 inches square.

In areas where summer temperatures are moderate, this cooling system will suffice, but in areas where temperatures range from 95°F and up in the summer months, the pad system is strongly recommended.

All of the calculations for heating and cooling are merely estimates. These formulas can be adapted for almost any area and will give satisfactory results. You can check the suppliers list for sources publishing more specific or detailed information.

Shading

In areas where temperatures exceed 85°F in the warmer months, for most plants it will be necessary to shade the building during this period. A shade that will eliminate 40 percent of the sunlight is recommended. There are a number of coatings that can be applied by either spray or brush, but you will probably find most of these somewhat unsatisfactory, especially when you start to remove them. I much prefer a shadecloth such as those available from some of the suppliers listed. These are woven to allow the required amount of light to penetrate and can be taken off and stored through the winter months.

Irrigation Timing and Gravel

When small seedlings or other young plants are first set out in the beds (using gravel medium), timers should be adjusted to irrigate the beds at 10:00 A.M. and 3:30 P.M. In warmer areas an additional feeding may be necessary. If so, irrigation times should be at 8:00 A.M., 12 noon, and 4:00 P.M. When the plants have been in the beds about three weeks, timers should be reset for normal growing procedures. In the winter months, two irrigations a day, one in the morning and one in the afternoon, should be sufficient. Through the warmer months or in areas where outside temperatures are high, the plants may require as many as four or five irrigations a day. If four seedings are made, they should be set as follows: 8:00 A.M., 11:00 A.M., 2:00 P.M., and 5:00 P.M. After you become more familiar with operating your system and begin to recognize the plants' needs, you can adjust your timing device accordingly. As given, these schedules are the norm for most vegetables and flowers.

For cucumbers, particularly in the warm months, six to seven irrigations a day are recommended. For strawberries, once a day should suffice. You should remember that more plants have been killed by overwatering than by underwatering.

Irrigation Sensors

One device that I introduced to hydroponic culture, which has contributed to my success as a grower is the electronic sensor. This sensor is used to actuate the sump-pumps. The triggering action is based on the amount of moisture in the growing beds. When the moisture content of the medium drops to approximately 30 percent, the plants will be near the wilting point. At this point the pumps will start. This, in effect, lets the plants determine when they need water.

Timers will give satisfactory results, but part of the time these cycles are incorrect. As an example, with three preset pumping cycles on a cloudy, cool day, the plants receive too much water; on a hot, sunny day three cycles may not be enough.

Because of the cost, however, the sensor is not recommended for the backyard grower or hobbyist.

It is extremely important that the surface of the gravel be kept dry. The beds should be filled to the proper level so that as the solution is pumped into the gravel the overflow system will function to drain off any excess. This leaves the top inch of gravel dry. You should check occasionally during irrigation cycles to see that the beds are filling properly.

In a gravel medium when the seedlings are first put into the beds, leave the same solution in the tank for two weeks. Then after this period, you should change the solution weekly. At the end of a crop cycle, when it is estimated that the crop will be taken out of the growing beds within 30 days, go back to a 10-day solution change. When the solution is discharged from the unit, it is still high in nutritional value and is excellent for use on a lawn, shrubbery, or other plants. By attaching a hose to the discharge pipe, you can distribute this solution where needed and will be pleased with the results. Adjust the pH to approximately 6.5 before pumping the solution out.

Irrigation Timing and Sand Culture

For sand culture, pumping cycles are not needed as often as in gravel. In the cool months the solution should be pumped to the plants twice a week. In the hot, dry summer months, it will be necessary to increase the irrigation cycles. By observing the plants, watching for wilting or hunger signs, you will be able to adjust to the correct cycles.

Thermostats and Heating

When adjusting thermostats to control the environment within the greenhouse, the following settings for tomatoes, cucumbers, lettuce, and most other crops are acceptable. Heating thermostats should be adjusted so a minimum temperature of 58°F is maintained at night. During periods of cloudy, cold weather, heating thermostats should be reset so a temperature of 70°F is maintained during the daylight hours. Humidistats should be set so that the humidity control fan is actuated when the humidity reaches 60 or 70 percent.

Thermostats and Cooling

For cooling, the thermostats controlling the exhaust fans or coolers should be set so that they are actuated when the temperature reaches 70°F. If a two-stage system is used, the first stage would be set at 70°F and the second at 75°F. Through the summer months, particularly in areas subject to high temperatures, settings should be at 60°F. If two stages are used, set one at 60°F and the other at 65°F. During this period the heaters should be cut off entirely.

In the more elaborate systems, a humidistat can be wired into the line controlling the pump that circulates water on the cooling pad. If you have this type of control, you should set this humidistat so the pump will not operate when the humidity levels in the greenhouse exceed 70 percent.

Placement of Thermostats

The thermostats controlling the heaters should be installed 3 to 4 feet from the front door. Lay the conduit on the floor, run it to the desired location and bend it upward at a 90-degree angle near the front edge of bed, 18 inches above the floor. Cooling thermostats and humidistats should be near the center of the building. Suspend them from the roof with the conduit over the inner edge of growing bed, 5 feet above the floor, facing north. Shade them with a small piece of plywood or other material so that direct sunlight does not strike the sensors.

In extremely hot, dry areas such as the Southwest, humidity levels may fall below minimum ranges for good pollination of tomatoes. This may be alleviated by doing the pollination in the early morning. It may be necessary in some areas to increase the humidity within the greenhouse by actuating the pumps. In extreme cases use a hose to wet down the walkways to create a more humid atmosphere. Pollination of tomatoes should never be done when the humidity is below 60 percent.

Various instruments are available for measuring humidity levels (see suppliers list). The grower who wants optimum production, particularly of tomatoes, must have these instruments.

Ready-built Systems

For the grower who does not wish to build his own greenhouse or hydroponic system, there are ready-built systems available (see suppliers list). There are also a number of companies that manufacture small greenhouses that the grower can equip with his own hydroponic equipment. All of these manufacturers can furnish buildings properly equipped with both heating and cooling systems designed to control temperatures in most areas.

This is an automated and completely self-contained system ready to plant. (Courtesy of Sturdi Products — see Suppliers List.)

Building Your Own Greenhouse: Step-by-Step Plans

The basic plan for this greenhouse was adapted from an original design by the Virginia Polytechnic Institute and State University, but I have suggested changes that are beneficial for the following reasons:

- Higher side walls and longer length make it easier to work in the building. More important, however, temperatures can be better controlled, especially for cooling.
- The added room allows for a larger plant population, a greater variety of plants, and the room to grow regular potted plants, orchids, etc.

MATERIALS FOR 12 X 20-FOOT GREENHOUSE

Lumber

2 pieces plywood ½" x 3' x 8' (for bow jig)
2 pieces pine or fir 2" x 4" x 6' for jig blocks
2 pieces redwood 2" x 6" x 14' (rip into lath for bows)
6 pieces redwood 2" x 4" x 6' (rip into 2" x 2" for blocks)

1 piece pine or fir 1" x 2" x 6' for blocks
 4 pieces redwood 1" x 2" x 14' for diagonal braces
 2 pieces redwood 2" x 4" x 20' for sills
 2 pieces redwood 2" x 4" x 12' for sills
 2 pieces redwood 1" x 4" x 20' for ridge boards
13 pieces redwood 2" x 4" x 8' for studs, braces,
     and stringers

Foundation

Concrete—2 cubic yards, 5-sack mix.
Lumber—1" x 6" or 2" x 6" as required for forming.
 2 pieces reinforcing rod 3/8" x 20'
 2 pieces reinforcing rod 3/8" x 12'
18 anchor bolts, 3/8" x 6", W-nuts, and washers

Hardware and Miscellaneous

6 pounds 6 d common cement-coated box nails
2 pounds 12 d common box nails
1 aluminum storm door 2',8" x 6',8"
1 quart white wood glue
PVC film or corrugated and flat fiberglass as cited.
Approximately 700 sq. ft. needed. If film is used, 6 pounds
     3 d box nails are needed.
For fiberglass, 5-ounce material is recommended.
Follow supplier's recommendation for nails and closure
     strips.
Cooling and heating equipment—sized for location and
     local climate (see suppliers list for sources).

For All Units

- Timer on the sump pumps (24 hr. so it may be set at different times depending on weather and time of year.)
- Thermostat for the heaters

Finished greenhouse is spacious, sturdy, and designed to operate efficiently in any climate.

For Unit Using "Pulling-Air" System

- Exhaust fans for front of the unit (with louvres)
- Pump for cooling-pad, sump-tank
- Humidistat
- Small exhaust fan to move air from the house (timer or humidistat)

For Unit Using "Pushing-Air" System

- 2 evaporative air coolers
- Thermostat
- Pumps for evaporative coolers (may come with coolers)
- Humidistat

NOTE: Mount 1 inch plywood board on front panel of unit to use as mounting board for timers, etc.

THE FOUNDATION

Lay out the foundation to the desired size. Set the outer form square and level.

Excavate for footing, 10 inches wide x 8 inches deep. Set the inner form, stake in place. Wire the forming boards together to prevent spreading. Use spacer blocks to ensure uniform width.

Approximately 2 yards of concrete are required (5-sack mix). Use 3/8 inch reinforcing rod. Place one rod parallel in the forms near the bottom while pouring the concrete. Set second rod parallel approximately 2 inches from the top of pour. Insert anchor bolts as shown in figure 16.

Step 1

Cut 2 pieces of ½-inch plywood to dimensions as shown in figure. Use 6-inch wide strips of same material to join. Nail securely at the joint.

Step 2

To construct and assemble bows, cut all material to dimensions as listed above. Redwood is recommended. If pine or fir is used, treat with wood preservative. Do *not* use creosote. Pentachlorophenols or some of the other preservatives may be harmful to the plastic cover. It is safe to use a 2 percent copper naphthenate solution. Wood may be soaked in solution or solution may be brushed on. If brushed on, use several coats.

The best lath to use is made by ripping 2 x 6s lengthwise from 14-foot boards. Lath should be a full ¼-inch thick. Lath may be soaked overnight in water. This will facilitate bending it in place, and there will be less chance that it will break or split.

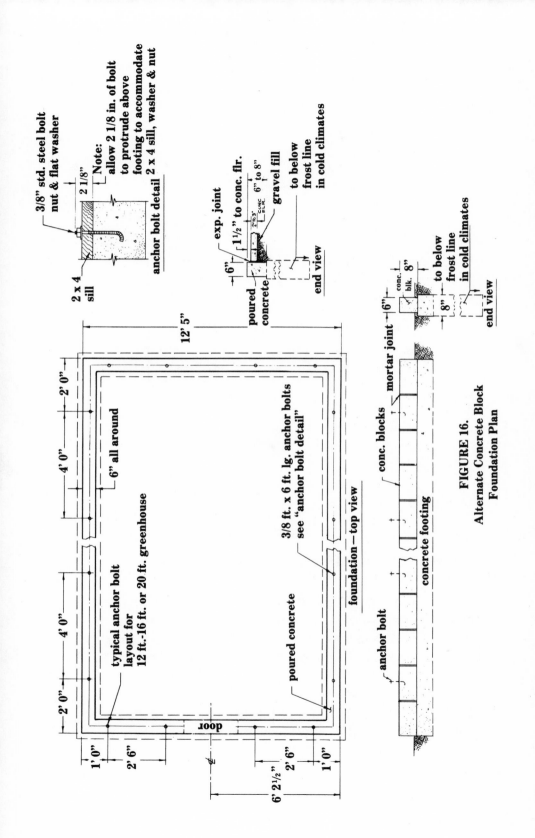

FIGURE 16.
Alternate Concrete Block
Foundation Plan

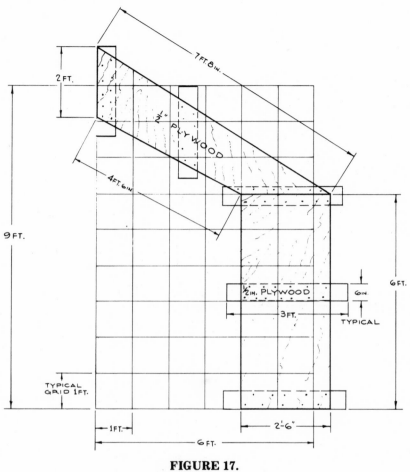

FIGURE 17.
STEP 1
Construction Layout For Bow Jig

From pine or fir 2 x 4s, cut and number 10 blocks in lengths as follows: no. 1, 6 inches; no. 2, 6 inches; no. 3, 4 inches; no. 4, 5 inches; no. 5, 9 inches; no. 6, 16 inches; no. 7, 9 inches; no. 8, 6½ inches; no. 9, 6 inches; and no. 10, 6 inches.

Place on plywood bow jig as shown and nail securely. With the exception of no. 1, blocks that do not fit square with the edge of the plywood will corner with the edge at

58

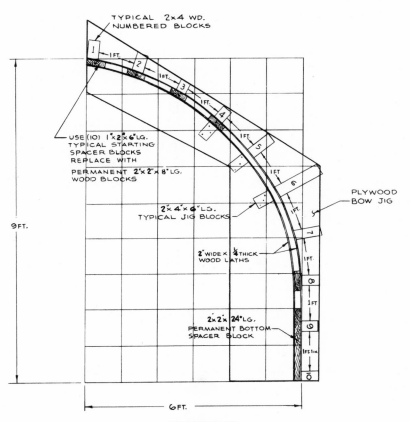

FIGURE 18.
STEP 2
Showing Completed Bow Jig & the Construction
of Bow Assembly

left. They will neither protrude or be slightly shorter on the right.

From 1 x 2-inch pine or fir, cut 10 blocks 6 inches in length for temporary spacing blocks.

Place lath against numbered 2 x 4 blocks, let ends extend evenly past blocks at the top and bottom. Starting at left top of jig, force lath against block no. 1. Tack 1 x 2 spacer block to hold lath against block. Continue around jig to right, forcing lath in place and holding by tacking 1 x 2 temporary spacers.

59

Cut 20 2 x 4 blocks 6 inches in length. Take a second piece of lath and place it against the temporary spacers. Starting at the upper left, force the lath against spacers using these 2 x 4 blocks. Nail the blocks securely to plywood.

Jig is now complete. Remove temporary 1 x 2 spacers. From 2 x 2-inch redwood, cut the following: 8 blocks 8 inches in length; 1 block 24 inches in length. These are the permanent spacer blocks. Coat the sides of these blocks with white wood glue and force between lath (as shown).

Nail securely with 6d coated nails. Allow glue to set till hard. Cut off excess lath at ends and remove bow from the jig. Continue to fabricate bows for required number. Twelve bows are needed for a 12 x 20-foot greenhouse.

Step 3

Lay bows out on the ground, and cut sill and ridge board to desired length. Drill holes in sill for foundation anchor bolts. Attach sill to bottom of bows with ¼ x 3-inch wood screws. Use spacing as shown. Attach ridge board (ridge plates) in same manner to top of bows.

When both halves are complete, raise and fasten ridge boards together. Recommended method of fastening ridge-boards is with ¼ x 2-inch bolts with washers and nuts.

Frame may now be set in place on foundation and bolted down.

Step 4

Cut 1 x 2-inch braces (length depends on size of the green-house) and insert from middle to ends as shown. Do not secure until the ends of the greenhouse are framed in and the greenhouse is plumbed.

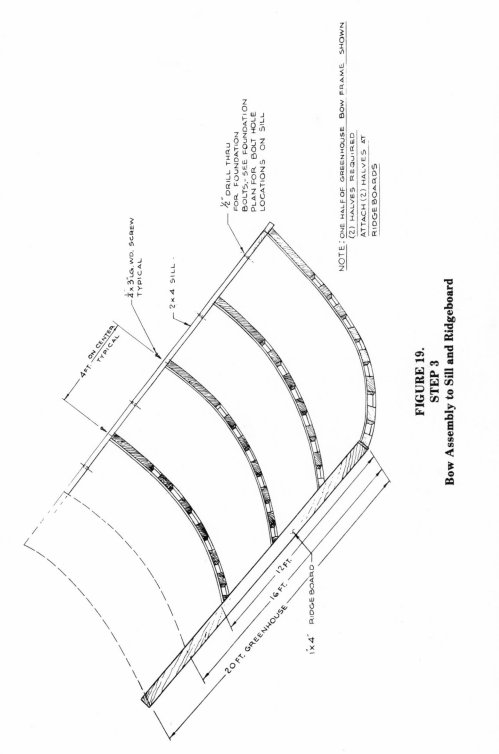

NOTE: ONE HALF OF GREENHOUSE BOW FRAME SHOWN
(2) HALVES REQUIRED
ATTACH (2) HALVES AT
RIDGE BOARDS

½" DRILL THRU
FOR FOUNDATION
BOLTS - SEE FOUNDATION
PLAN FOR BOLT HOLE
LOCATIONS ON SILL

¼ x 3" LG. WD. SCREW
TYPICAL

2 x 4 SILL

4 FT. ON CENTER
TYPICAL

12 FT.

16 FT.

20 FT. GREENHOUSE

1 x 4" RIDGE BOARD

FIGURE 19.
STEP 3
Bow Assembly to Sill and Ridgeboard

61

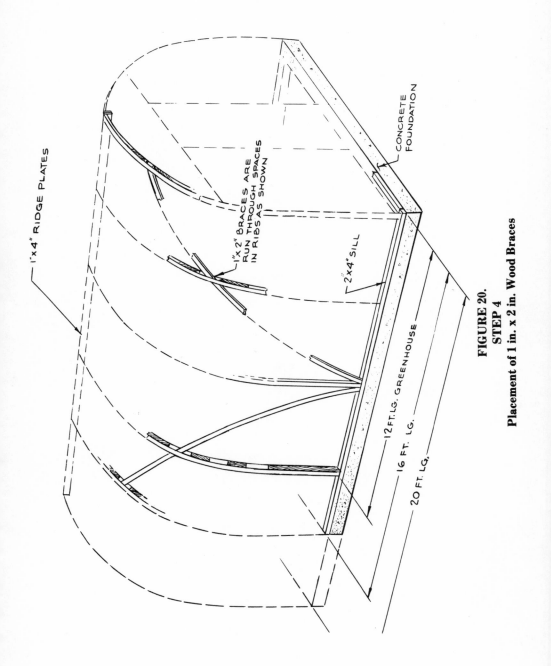

FIGURE 20.
STEP 4
Placement of 1 in. x 2 in. Wood Braces

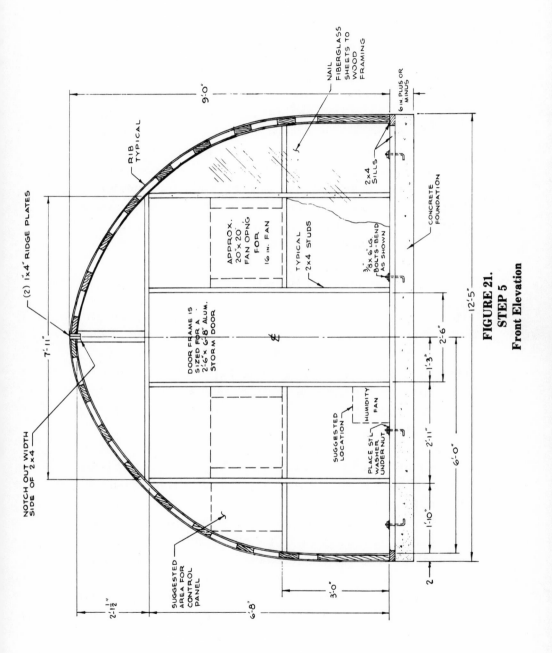

FIGURE 21.
STEP 5
Front Elevation

Step 5

Lay front sill in place and bolt down. Cut 4 2 x 4s for studs. Cut these 6 feet, 8 inches long.

Set in place as shown. Cut stringer to fit on top of studs. This stringer should measure 7 feet, 11 inches on top side and 8 feet, 2 inches on the bottom (slanted). This may vary slightly due to difference in curvature of bow. Check measurement carefully before cutting; fit and nail. Measure, cut, and nail balance of framing as shown.

Do not hang the door until the surfaces are covered and the greenhouse is plumbed (level and perpendicular). Openings for fans (or exhaust ports) should be framed to specs as shown by the manufacturer. If a humidity fan is to be installed, frame as specified.

Step 6

Frame and cover the greenhouse. Lay rear sill in place and bolt it down. Cut 2 2 x 4 studs 6 feet, 8 inches long. Cut 1 2 x 4 stringer 8 feet long; use at the bottom of the pad space. Stringer at the top of the pad space should measure 8 feet on the top side, 8 feet, 3 inches on the bottom (slanted). This measurement may vary because of bow curvature.

Check carefully before cutting; fit and nail in place. Measure and cut braces and other studs as shown. Plumb the greenhouse and fasten 1 x 2-inch diagonal braces (shown in figure 20).

With bows and framing in place, the greenhouse is ready for covering. If corrugated fiberglass panels are used on roof and sides, 5 to 7 panels (approximately 4 feet wide) will be needed, depending on the width of the panels. Length as desired. If this width is not available, 12 panels with 2-foot width coverage will be needed.

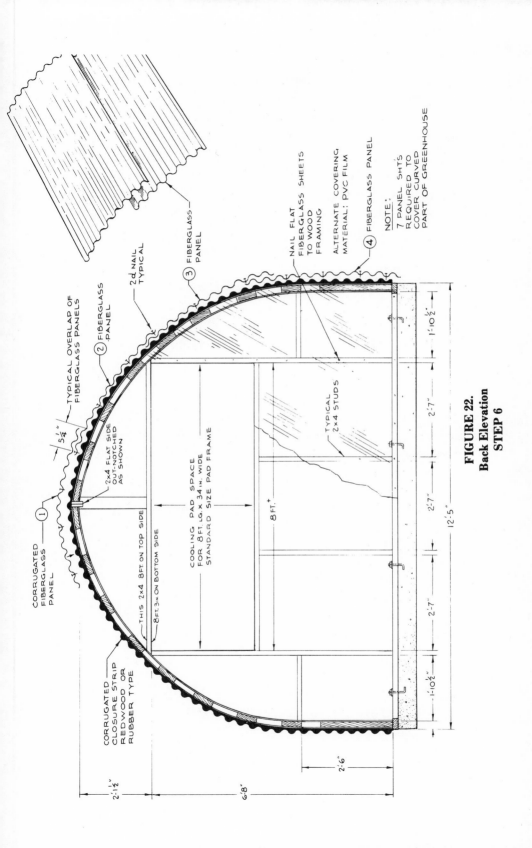

FIGURE 22.
Back Elevation
STEP 6

Tack corrugated closure strips to bows as shown in figure 22. Lay panel on top, lengthwise of greenhouse. Center this panel on ridge and nail in place using screw-type aluminum roofing nails with neoprene washers. Holes for nails should be predrilled. Do *not* nail edges so that the next panel may be inserted under the top panel and lapped properly as shown. Attach remaining panels the same way.

Cover the end walls with flat fiberglass. Drill and nail as with the corrugated panels (as shown). If film covering is used for the entire cover, 6 mil or heavier PVC film is recommended.

Film should be drawn taut over the bows, fastened by nailing 1 x $\frac{1}{4}$-inch lath over the film to bows and sills. Use small nails to prevent lath from splitting. Ends should be covered and fastened to framing in the same manner.

Step 7

Install door, fans (louvres), and cooling pad as shown in drawing. After the hydroponic beds and sump are in place and all plumbing is connected, it is recommended that a concrete floor 2 to 3 inches thick be poured.

Floor should be painted white. Light reflection from the white floor will be of considerable benefit to plants during periods of low light intensity. It will also enhance the appearance of the greenhouse.

Growing Media

There are many types of rooting media used in soilless culture. Gravel, sand, vermiculite, hadite, and pumice are some of the ones more commonly used.

Gravel

It is my opinion, based on tests conducted over the past 15 years, that gravel is a superior rooting medium for a number of reasons. In most areas usable gravel can be found, and it is much easier to clean and sterilize than any other medium. One of the problems encountered with all of the various types of growing media, however, is the buildup of salts. In areas where the salt content of the raw water is high, this buildup can occur very rapidly.

Even in water that is virtually free of many elements, the addition of the plant nutrient will cause a surprisingly fast accumulation of the various salts such as nitrates, chlorides, and others. Using gravel, these salts can be leached out quickly with minimal labor. It is much harder, however, to rid sand of these elements, through leaching, and with vermiculite or the peat-lite mixes, it is necessary to put in a completely new mix at the end of each crop. Hadite, cinders, and similar materials can be used but are usually recommended only as a last resort when you cannot obtain good gravel.

The selection of the right kind and size of gravel is of extreme importance. Crushed rock can be used, but round, smooth, river-type gravel is highly preferable. Calcerous gravel should not be used since the leaching of lime into the solution will make it virtually impossible for you to maintain a correct pH level. It will also cause the nutrient solution to constantly go out of balance.

If at all possible, you should have the gravel tested by a competent laboratory, unless you are absolutely positive that the gravel is clean and contains no impurities or elements that will leach into the solution. Because of their hardness, most of the granitic types of gravel are best.

If the only gravel available contains some calcerous substances, it can be treated with Treble Super Phosphate. Even after treating, however, this type of gravel, will never be as productive as the granitic type. Smooth, rounded gravels are best because each time the growing medium is flooded, the gravel is coated with an invisible film containing the various elements in the nutrient solution. This film will adhere to a smooth, rounded stone much better than to one that is rough or cracked. The sharp edges of crushed stone can also injure the root system.

The size of the gravel should be neither smaller than ¼ inch in diameter nor larger than ½ inch. Use all possible care in washing the gravel to be sure it contains no soil, clay, dirt, or debris of any kind. After it is thoroughly washed and placed in the growing beds or troughs, you are ready to begin sterilizing it.

Flood the beds with fresh water to which enough sulphuric acid (muriatic acid may be used) has been added to lower the pH to the 3.0 to 4.0 range. Be sure that the gravel is completely flooded and covered with this acid bath. This solution should be left in the gravel for at least 12 hours. Then flush the gravel thoroughly with fresh water. Add a fresh solution containing one quart of Clorox (or 14 percent swimming pool liquid chlorine) per 100 gallons of water. This solution should be left covering the gravel for at least 6 hours. Completely drain and flush thoroughly with clear water at least twice.

This same treatment should be followed at the end of each crop cycle. This procedure is absolutely essential if the water supply contains more than 100 ppm of total salts such as sodium, magnesium, nitrates, and others. Many growers whose first crops were extremely successful have had succeeding crops that produced far less because of this salt buildup.

One of the reasons for the use of gravel is the fine aeration obtained, as compared to sand or other growing media. Another reason gravel is a superior growing medium is that each time the nutrient is pumped into the gravel, the stale air from which most of the oxygen has been lost is forced out. Some CO_2 will also be forced out, which is beneficial to plant growth.

When the pump (or pumps) are cut off, the solution will return to the sump-tank by gravity flow. As it leaves the gravel, it creates something of a vacuum, and this action draws fresh air through the voids in the gravel, furnishing fresh oxygen to the root system.

It is advisable to flush gravel with fresh water occasionally during a crop cycle. Once a month is sufficient if water with a low total salt content is used. If the salt content of the raw water is high, flushing the gravel from the top with a hose twice a month will improve production. Water used to flush out the gravel must be pumped out of the system before mixing a new nutrient solution.

Sand

If you cannot find a suitable gravel and are forced to turn to sand (or if you prefer the sand culture method of hydroponics), you should exercise much care in selecting the sand to be used. You should have tests made of the sand to be sure it is noncalcerous and free of other elements that would affect plant growth. The sand should be washed clean of soil and debris of any kind.

It is extremely important in sand culture to use a type of sand that does not pack too tightly when either dry or wet. A sand that will pack or settle into a tight cohesive mass will eliminate much of the aeration needed around the root system. Granitic type sands are best.

One of the major problems in finding the right type of sand is that many deposits of sand on beaches, along rivers, or in dry stream beds have been laid down in a more or less stratified manner. This leaves layers of silt in the deposits. Much of this silt will be scattered throughout the sand, requiring thorough washing. After it has been cleaned and put in the growing beds, the sand should be washed from the top to leach out any remaining unwanted elements.

It is a good practice to wash the sand from the top every three or four weeks throughout a crop cycle because build-up of various elements from the nutrient will occur much more rapidly than in gravel culture. Leach the sand thoroughly at the end of each crop cycle before replanting. If neither suitable sand nor gravel is available or if you prefer to use a vermiculite or peat-lite mix, I suggest that you write to Cornell University (see suppliers list). Dr. Raymond Sheldrake of Cornell is known the world over for his work in growing vegetables in various types of peat-lite mixes, and many growers have enjoyed success by using the different mixes he has developed. Unless it is dried and properly sterilized at the end of a crop cycle, you will be far better off discarding the old mix and starting each crop with a new mix, although some growers report satisfactory results using the same mix for two crops.

The Nutrient Solution and Plant Nutrition

Any plant grower, whether a complete novice or an experienced grower, must realize that a growing plant is a living entity. Its nutritional needs and the manner in which it assimilates food are very complex. It takes in food through both the root system and the foliage. Although most plants will live on the same plant foods, some plants require more or less of certain elements if optimum growth is to be obtained. The differences in available sunlight and changes in temperature and humidity have a decided effect on the intake by plants of the various elements they are fed. The plant will assimilate and use varying amounts of nutritional elements at different times of the year. The normal behavior of most plants is to grow, flower, and produce in the spring and summer. They then go into a dormant or semidormant condition in the fall and winter.

The tomato plant is a good example. It is necessary to feed the plant rather heavily in the early spring to achieve vigorous growth and flowering. As it becomes warmer and the first four or five of the heavier clusters of fruit have been set on the vine, the amount of nutrient used in the solution should be decreased. This is usually about the time the first fruit is being harvested. By May or June, temperatures in most areas in the northern hemisphere are more conducive to good plant growth. With longer days and more bright sunshine, food intake by the plant is excellent and all of the elements in the nutrient solution are readily absorbed by the plant.

Forced Feeding

When tomato plants are set in a greenhouse for a fall and winter crop, the reverse is true. In the fall of the year, as the daylight hours become progressively shorter and cooler weather begins to set in, the plants will not take into their growing systems the needed elements as fast as in spring and summer. At this point it is necessary to begin to increase the concentration of the solution.

In the winter months, the available sunlight is at its lowest point. In most areas this period of the year is accompanied by overcast skies, which results in a further reduction of the amount of light available to plants. Temperatures are at their lowest ranges. All growers know that even with a controlled environment growth will begin to slow down.

Production will drop, and fruit will ripen much slower. This can be offset only by heavier feeding of the plant. If you are using a teaspoon of plant food per gallon of water or a pound per 100 gallons in the warm months, and if you are to achieve anything like satisfactory production, it will be necessary to almost double these amounts through the winter months.

One way to offset slower ripening and improve production is by keeping the temperature of the nutrient solution at or near 70°F by using a heating coil or similar device in the sump-tank. The temperature of the solution should never be allowed to drop below 60°F. A number of growers have questioned me about why their tomatoes were not ripening. In every instance this problem was due to the low temperature of the solution. This can also cause other problems such as bullish growth and poor fruit set.

As weather conditions begin to improve, you can begin to cut back the amount of plant food used in the solution mix. By summer you will be feeding your plants only half as much as in the winter, in some areas even less. At the end of the summer season, as you start the new fall crop, you should again begin increasing the nutrient concentration.

When increasing the salt concentration of the nutrient solution, you must be careful because if this concentration becomes too high, the plants will wilt. If the condition is not corrected, leaf burn and blossom drop will be noticeable, and eventually the plants will die. This condition seems to be more prevalent in the warmer months, particularly in areas with intense light. The best remedy is to immediately pump out the solution tank and flush out the gravel with fresh water, thus leaching any excess salts out of the growing medium. Refill the tank with water. Do not add nutrient for two or three days. Pump this water out, refill the tank, and use a lower salt concentration in your nutrient mix.

Although it is theoretically possible under forced conditions for a plant to produce as much in the fall and winter as in the spring and summer, I have yet to see this theory borne out in actual practice. Most growers will find that if they are able to produce half as much from a given number of plants in the fall and winter as they did in the spring and summer, they have done an excellent job.

pH Control

In mixing the nutrient solution, the first step is to adjust the pH of the raw water being used. pH values range from 1.0 to 14.0. The neutral point is 7.0. A pH below 7.0 is acid, above 7.0 is alkaline. One point to remember is that a pH of 7.0 is 10 times that of a pH of 6.0. C. E. Ticquet, in his excellent work *Successful Gardening Without Soil*, expressed the need for a correct pH range better than anyone. He wrote, "If you ask for one lump of sugar in your tea, you do not expect to get 10. If you do it may sicken you and this is exactly what happens to plants!"

A pH between 5.8 and 6.2 is considered best for most plants. I cannot overemphasize the fact that *before* any of the various salts or plant food is mixed with the raw water, the pH must be adjusted to the correct level. If the water is on the alkaline side, carrying a pH value of 8.0, and you mix in the various salts without first adjusting the pH, you will have an immediate loss of iron and possibly other elements that are vital to good plant growth. Depending on what elements may be in the raw water, you may also have a lockup of other elements, which means that the plant cannot assimilate them even though they are there. Although they remain in the solution, they will not be available to the plant.

A roll of nitrazine paper can be used in testing the pH. This can be purchased at almost any pharmacy or drug store. The small test kit used by pool owners is adequate. More accurate testing equipment is available, however, for growers who want it (see suppliers list).

If the equipment uses only a few gallons of solution, two regular aspirin tablets per gallon of water will lower a pH of 8.0 to near 6.0. A teaspoon or so of distilled white vinegar will also produce the same results and may be used in most home units for controlling the pH.

For large and commercial systems, sulphuric acid should be used. When using acid, *always pour the acid into the water, never pour water into the acid.* If you inadvertently splatter or pour acid on yourself, wash immediately with fresh water to avoid severe burns. To adjust the pH of a larger amount of raw water, you should slowly pour in a small amount of acid, stir the water thoroughly and then test again. Continue to do this until the correct pH level is obtained. After a little experience, you will know approximately how much acid to add each time.

For water with a pH below 5.5, it will be necessary to raise the pH level. Although a higher pH is normal in most waters, occasionally water will be found with a pH below 5.8. This is usually the case in the southeastern part of the

United States. Potassium hydroxide is most often used to buffer water with a low pH. Sodium hydroxide can also be used. Hydroxides are caustic and should be used with care. They should *never* be handled with wet hands. You should begin by adding small amounts, then stir and test thoroughly until the suitable level is reached. Once you have determined how much is needed per gallon or per 100 gallons, it is a fairly simple matter to adjust the solution thereafter.

Daily checks of the pH levels should be made and the pH adjusted as necessary. The following are the recommended ranges and levels, and should not be exceeded. The optimum pH is the center figure given.

Tomato	5.8 — 6.2 — 6.4
Bean	"
Pepper	"
Radish	"
Gladiolus	"
Strawberry	"
Rose	"
Cucumber	5.5 — 6.3 — 6.5
Lettuce	"
Eggplant	5.5 — 6.0
Cabbage	6.0 — 6.5 — 7.0
Celery	"
Pea	"
Asparagus	"
Chrysanthemum	"
Sweet Pea	
Melon	5.0 — 5.5 — 6.0
Amaryllis	"

As you can see with this chart, there is not a great difference in ranges. All of these crops would be compatible. The pH should be adjusted for the principal crop grown, in order to achieve optimum production from it. Satisfactory results should be gained from the others.

Once the pH level of the raw water in the solution tank has been adjusted to the correct level, stir in the nutrient. Some of the elements going into these nutrient mixes are often hard to dissolve. If this is the case, pour the needed amount of nutrient into a small container of water from the solution tank and mix as thoroughly as possible. Then pour the solution into the tank and be sure it is thoroughly mixed and stirred. With most of the nutrient mixes, especially in large tanks, the operator will achieve better results by stirring the solution daily.

The average grower will probably have more success buying a ready-mixed plant food. There are a number of companies that manufacture premixed nutrients (see suppliers list.) (If you wish to mix your own nutrient, see formulas on page 82.) I have used and tested most of those available in the United States and do not find a great deal of difference between them. I have also found that they work with varying results, depending on climatic conditions. There may also be a large difference in results because of the various elements found in the raw water. I have yet to find any nutrient that will not need certain additives at different stages in the plant growth. The most common deficiencies are iron and magnesium, although the plants will occasionally show other deficiencies such as calcium, manganese, boron, and others.

Nutrient Deficiencies and Control

The most common deficiency noted in most plants is lack of *iron*. This is also one of the easiest to recognize. This will be noted first in the young growth in the top of the plant. This new growth begins to pale and if the condition is allowed to continue, the leaves in the tops of the plants will bleach and show a decided chlorosis. Some scorching of the leaf tips and margins may also occur. Blossom drop will occur on fruiting plants such as tomatoes. This condition in tomatoes usually becomes most evident at about the time the fourth or fifth clusters of fruit start to develop. At this point, with a heavy load of fruit much of the iron in the nutrient is diverted from the entire plant to the fruit. Thus starvation of the new growth occurs near the top. In hydroponic tomato culture, it is usually good practice to begin to *add small amounts of iron* to the solution at the time the second and third clusters are well set. In this manner you may often avert bloom drop on later clusters.

Another common deficiency is lack of *magnesium*. On most plants mottling will appear on the older, heavier leaves at the bottom of the plant. As the deficiency increases, these leaves may also begin to roll upward. The yellow mottling will continue to spread, and eventually the yellow spots will turn brown or become necrotic and the leaves will begin to wither. When the deficiency becomes extremely acute, the entire foliage of the plant will appear yellow and mottled. Only the new growth at the very tip of the plant will remain green. This deficiency can be corrected by the addition of *magnesium sulphate* to the solution, calculated at 1 teaspoon per gallon, or ½ pound per 100 gallons. The most common form of magnesium sulphate is *epsom salts*. Even quicker results in correcting this deficiency may be obtained by *spraying* the plants with a solution of 2 tablespoons of *epsom salts* in a gallon of water. Two or three sprayings spaced two days apart will usually result in a marked improvement in the color of the leaves.

Calcium deficiency is also very common. This is often brought on by water stress during a hot, dry period where there is a high loss of moisture by the plant through transspiration. This condition almost invariably occurs after a period of cloudy, rainy weather followed by bright sunshine and warmer temperatures. In tomatoes large brown spots will appear on the blossom end of the fruit, which begins to decay very rapidly. This is commonly known as blossom-end rot and can be corrected very quickly by *spraying* the plant with a solution of 4 tablespoons of *calcium chloride* in one gallon of water. Three applications of this spray made every other day will usually suffice. It may also be necessary to add some calcium—either *calcium chloride* or *calcium nitrate*—to the solution. In severe cases of calcium deficiency, growing points are killed and bloom-drop occurs, and the root system will be very poorly developed.

Another condition brought on by cloudy, humid period followed by bright sunshine is *wilting*. During an extended occurrence of cloudy weather, the plant becomes soft and in effect, water logged. Hot sunshine will cause some wilting between feedings. This condition will usually right itself in four or five days as growth slows down and the plants harden.

Under these same conditions, you will find some fruit damage from *splitting* or *cracking*. This can be stopped by *misting the plants* with a solution made of 1 teaspoon of *table salt* per gallon of water. Apply this spray three times, one day apart. Salt added to the nutrient solution at the rate of 1 teaspoon per gallon, or 1 pound per hundred gallons, may be used as an alternative remedy. It should not be necessary to use this salt treatment longer than one week, and the treatment should not be used at all if the raw water has a high sodium content.

Nitrogen deficiency is found occasionally, although in hydroponic farming it is not seen too often. With a nitrogen deficiency, the entire plant becomes dwarfed, pale and thin, and there may be places tinged with purple. The older leaves will yellow and dry up. One very obvious symptom, particularly in tomato plants, is that the leaves in the new growth appear to stand up in a vertical position. The addi-

78

tion of *ammonium nitrate* to the solution will correct this deficiency.

In *phosphorus* deficiency, plant growth is thin and dwarfed. The leaves will curl backward, showing a pronounced droop with a dull purple tint. Often a switch from sulphuric acid to *phosphoric* acid in maintaining the pH will correct a phosphorus deficiency.

Another fairly common deficiency in many plants, particularly of the vegetable family, is lack of *boron*. This problem is somewhat harder to diagnose than the others. Again, using a tomato plant as an example, the first symptoms can be detected in the top of the plant. The plant begins to get a heavy, brushy growth in the top with a decided twirl. If the main stem of the plant is examined closely, it will usually be found to have separated completely in places, or there may be indented areas in the stem. By splitting the stem lengthwise with a sharp knife, brown spots will be found in the core and will be corklike in appearance. The leaves may become highly colored with purple, red, and yellow tints. There may be pits in the skin of the fruit. For some unknown reason, when this deficiency occurs in the earlier stages of the crop, the plants will recover of their own accord. The addition of minute amounts of *boric acid* will correct this problem.

You may encounter still other deficiencies in plants. Many of these are hard to diagnose without a tissue analysis. Most colleges and universities and some independent laboratories will run these tests for you. They normally charge a fixed fee for each element requested in the test.

The most common deficiency found in lettuce is lack of *calcium*. This causes the leaf margins to scorch or turn brown and is commonly known as tip burn. The addition of *calcium nitrate* to the solution will correct this.

One word of caution: in making a visual diagnosis you should exercise care to be as certain as possible that your plants have a particular deficiency. There are several toxicities affecting plants that have characteristics almost identical to some of the deficiencies. If the grower has a toxicity and treats it as a deficiency, he may worsen the problem. There are many excellent publications covering plant deficiencies published by different agricultural universities.

One condition that often occurs in tomatoes, while not classed as a normal deficiency, should be mentioned. This is commonly described as *mealiness* and is usually noted as the first fruit begins to ripen. When sliced, the tomato will not be as firm as it should be and often will not have the taste or flavor expected. This condition can be corrected quickly by sharply increasing or decreasing the amount of nutrient. In the spring and summer, I recommend that the concentration be doubled for one week, then gradually reduced for the next two weeks until it is brought back to normal strength for that period of the year. In the winter months, when the solution strength is normally double that of the summer months, I recommend that it be reduced to half strength for one week, then brought back to full strength in the following two weeks. By following this procedure, the condition should be eliminated within a week to 10 days.

Both the average commercial grower and hobbyist will usually achieve better results by purchasing a premixed nutrient (see suppliers list). One recent development that has been of great benefit to hydroponic growers is the process used by many manufacturers of chelating or altering various elements. A good example of this is iron. Ferrous sulphate is called for in most of the older formulas. Iron in a chelated form goes into solution more readily and is less likely to precipitate. Many of the other elements used in a hydroponic formula are also chelated and in this form become more available to the plants. If mixing a formula, a hydroponic grower should use chelated elements if they are available.

80

Organic vs. Hydroponic Growing

Something I have often been asked about is the difference between organic gardening and hydroponics. Some people have even said that they would not eat vegetables grown hydroponically because the grower used chemicals to grow the plants. What must be understood is that these so-called chemicals are the purest form of inorganic elements. The organic gardener uses manures and composts made of decayed vegetable matter for fertilizer. What many do not understand is that before any element such as nitrogen can become available to the root system of the plant, it must break down into an inorganic form. There is no question that these organic fertilizers are good. In the opinion of most authorities, however, the inorganic forms are much purer. When mixed into the soil or used in hydroponic gardening, they will be taken up by the plant much more quickly. This results in a healthier, heavier producing plant. People eating hydroponic vegetables grown with the use of inorganic elements are far less likely to pick up amoeba or other harmful bacteria. Anyone who has ever seen a hydroponic unit being operated properly must agree that this type of farming is certainly superior in sanitation and cleanliness. The main point to remember is that regardless of how much manure or other material is mixed into the soil, the plant being fed will receive no benefits whatsoever until the various elements have broken down into inorganic form.

Nutrient Formulas To Mix

For the small grower who wishes to mix his own formula, I recommend this one developed by Texas A&M University. It will give excellent results.

Step I   *For each 5 gallons of water add:*

    1 teaspoon of monopotassium phosphate
    1 teaspoon of sodium nitrate
    2½ teaspoons of magnesium sulphate
    1 teaspoon of calcium chloride
    (This is the nutrient solution.)

Step II   *To prepare the micro-nutrients,*
    dissolve in ½ gallon of water the following:

    1 teaspoon boric acid
    1 teaspoon of manganese sulphate
    1/8 teaspoon of copper sulphate
    1 teaspoon of zinc sulphate

Add 1 to 2 teaspoons of the micro-nutrient solution to each 5 gallons of nutrient solution.

Step III Dissolve ¼ teaspoon of ferric chloride in one pint of water and add 7 tablespoons of this solution for each 5 gallons of nutrient solution.

The formula below is from *Successful Gardening Without Soil,* by C. E. Ticquet (converted to U. S. measurements).

Step I   *For each 100 gallons of water:*

    7¼ oz. potassium nitrate
    8¼ oz. sodium nitrate
    1¾ oz. ammonium sulphate
    6 oz. monocalcium phosphate
    7 oz. magnesium sulphate
    11½ oz. calcium sulphate

Plus micro-nutrients as follows:

Step II *In 5 gallons of water dissolve:*

> 2 oz. of iron sulphate
> ¼ oz. of manganese sulphate
> ⅓ oz. of boric acid
> 1/10 oz. of zinc sulphate
> 1/20 oz. of copper sulphate

Add 2 quarts of this solution to each 100 gallons of nutrient solution.

If you observe deficiencies while using either of these formulas or others, the following amounts of the more common elements used are recommended:

Iron—1½ oz. chelated iron per 1000 gallons of solution. For smaller amounts of solution a tiny pinch will be sufficient. You should be careful not to overcorrect this deficiency.

Boron—a very small amount should be used, based on 1 oz. per 1000 gallons.

Magnesium— ½ pound of epsom salts per 100 gallons, or 1 teaspoon per gallon.

Calcium—2 pounds of calcium nitrate per 1000 gallons, or 1 heaping teaspoon per 100 gallons.

Nitrogen—1 pound of ammonium nitrate per 1000 gallons or 1 teaspoon per 100 gallons.

Foliar Feeding

In addition to feeding the plant through the root system, I have increased production, particularly in tomatoes, through the use of foliar feeding. Using a small garden mister or a bottle with a fine-spray head, spray the foliage with the same solution used to feed the roots. In large commercial-sized houses, attach a small bilge pump to a common garden hose that is equipped with a water breaker, and place the bilge pump in the solution tank. Pressure type sprayers, holding 2 to 3 gallons, can also be used. *Never* use sprayers for weed killers, insecticides or other such sprays.

Two or three applications a week will have extremely beneficial results on the plants and will most certainly increase the fruit set and production. The plant should not be sprayed in this manner during rainy weather or when the skies are heavily overcast, however. Almost any deficiency can be corrected much more quickly through foliar feeding than through the root system. There are numerous systems available today for misting plants (see suppliers list). As a rule these misting systems are used to water the plants and lower temperatures. I feel that there will be much progress made in the near future with this method of giving plants more nutrition.

For *iron* and *manganese* foliar spray, mix as follows and use at three-day intervals a minimum of three times:

Iron—To one gallon of water add ½ teaspoon of Sequestrene (Giegy) 330.

Manganese—To one gallon of water add ½ teaspoon of manganese sulphate.

(Do *not* mix these two chemicals.)

CO_2

One aspect of nutrition that has not been covered is the enrichment of the greenhouse atmosphere through the use of carbon dioxide (CO_2). Growers the world over are aware that better production is gained through the use of CO_2, which "fertilizes" the atmosphere. When fresh air is brought into the greenhouse, the normal level of CO_2 is approximately 330 ppm (parts per million). Much research has been done in this field, and 1500 ppm is generally considered the optimum level. An increase to 700 or 800 ppm has been found to be very beneficial to all plants, particularly lettuce. Most of the CO_2 systems in use today are designed for the commercial grower. There are, however, instruments available to measure the CO_2 level in a greenhouse. If you wish to add CO_2 to the greenhouse atmosphere, you should certainly monitor the amount being introduced and should not increase these levels above 1500 ppm.

For the hobbyist who wishes to experiment in a small greenhouse, CO_2 may be purchased in containers and then dispersed into the greenhouse by cracking open the valve on the container. Some experimental work has, however, been done by sprinkling what is commonly called "dry ice" on the floor of the greenhouse.

CO_2 should be introduced into the greenhouse atmosphere in the cooler months when the exhaust fans are not operating and during daylight hours. The only time that CO_2 should be fed into the atmosphere at night is when you are using artificial lights. It is of no value to the plants unless there is enough light for photosynthesis.

Water Analysis

As mentioned earlier, the salt content of the raw water is an important factor in growing plants hydroponically, and you should have your water analyzed to determine its salt concentration. If you are using water from a city or other approved source, an analysis can be obtained from the water department. If the water is from a private source such as a well, you can check with the State Water Board, as it may have an analysis from the water table near your well. If these sources cannot furnish analysis, it will be necessary to have the water analyzed by a competent laboratory. The cost should not be excessive. If there is no laboratory available, a nearby university may be willing to perform this service.

An analysis will show the amounts of the various salts in water as parts per million (ppm). The combined total is shown as dissolved salts (DS). If this total is less than 700 ppm, use of this water should present no problems. If much higher, it may require some changes in the nutrient formula.

As an example of the need for a water analysis, if the water being used has a total of 700 ppm DS, the addition of the nutrient salts to the water will increase this by 1000 to 1400 ppm (because of the formula used). You then have a total concentration of 1700 to 2100 ppm. This concentration will increase further because of evaporation and other factors. In seven or eight days, concentration levels may reach the point where plant growth will be affected. This is one reason that dumping and recharging the solution on a weekly basis is recommended.

If this is not done, deficiencies or toxicities will appear. Although too expensive for the hobbyist, the researcher or commercial grower must have a DS meter (see suppliers list). This instrument will not identify the different salts but will accurately measure the total salt content and will indicate when to adjust or change the solution.

Sodium chloride, or plain salt, is one of the most common salts found in excessive amounts. Tomatoes, cucumbers, and lettuce are some of the plant species with a high salt tolerance. I have grown good crops of tomatoes using water with a total DS of 4400 ppm, most of which was sodium chloride. I have seen other good crops where these levels ranged from 2000 to 3000 ppm.

Tomatoes grown hydroponically using this kind of water will tend to have heavy stems and dark green foliage. Plants will be stocky in appearance but will produce well, although not as heavily as those grown with better water. By adding phosphorus, potassium, and nitrogen, better yields may be obtained. Use of sulphate salts such as calcium and magnesium should be limited or left out. The researcher or commercial grower should study *Guide to*

Commercial Hydroponics, by M. Schwarz (see suppliers list). The sections of this book dealing with saline waters are very good.

The ability to grow good crops in these waters again points up the need for hydroponics. In conventional farming, it would be almost impossible to grow profitable crops using such water without very expensive treatment. In hydroponics the amounts of water needed are far less, and treatment is both feasible and economical. Recent work in the reverse osmosis treatment of water with high mineral content is encouraging.

In areas with extremely high temperatures in the warm months, water loss will be high from transpiration and evaporation and will necessitate the addition of larger amounts of fresh water daily. If the salt content of the raw water is not excessive (500 ppm or less), you may be able to carry your solution for 2 weeks, particularly in the latter stages of the crop. If this is done, you should add half the amount of nutrient used in making up the beginning solution. This addition should be made at the end of the first week, and the entire solution should be dumped at the end of the second week.

In the winter months, excessive nitrogen intake may occur, especially in tomatoes. If this reaches toxic levels, leaves on the entire plant begin to yellow and loss of blossoms will occur. This can be corrected by dumping the solution. Add ½ pound of sugar per 100 gallons of water, and *do not* add any nutrient to this solution. By feeding the plants this sugared water for one week, nitrogen levels in the plant tissue will be reduced and recovery should be rapid. Some loss of acid in the fruit will be noticed and the flavor will be much sweeter.

Plant Care

Once the hydroponic system is built, the beds sterilized and checked for leaks, and the pumps, timers and other equipment are checked to see that they are functioning properly, you are ready to plant.

Plant Compatibility

Since most of my work has been with tomatoes, cucumbers, and lettuce, I will deal primarily with these plants. One of the first steps you should take is to determine the best temperature and humidity levels for the plants that you wish to grow in your greenhouse. Most of the vegetable varieties are more or less compatible and will thrive in the same environment. For the hobbyist, in a small home unit, a number of vegetables can be grown simultaneously. Although some of these may not produce at optimum levels, they will produce satisfactorily.

Some vegetables can be grown more easily in the winter months with a minimum amount of sunlight and at fairly low temperatures. With most of these plants, growth and production will be accelerated by making the plants more comfortable and growing them at warmer temperatures.

Tomatoes

In growing tomatoes, the first consideration is the seedling. A good seedling is an absolute must if you wish to have a successful crop. There are many different methods used in growing seedlings. A number of types of pots and growing blocks are available. I have produced the best seedlings by using blocks made of cellulose fibers or the compressed type of peat. The first is known under the trade name of "BR8" or "Gro Blocks," the latter as "Kys" cubes (see suppliers list). For tomatoes either type of growing block is excellent for use in gravel or other inert media. For lettuce I much prefer the "BR8." With these blocks planting is very easy.

Seedlings

When watering seed blocks, use lukewarm water to speed germination. The blocks also should be kept warm, if at all possible. Heated propagation mats are available and are used by many growers. One grower I know uses a heating pad (set on low) under a tray of seedling blocks to accelerate germination and growth.

I recommend that you drop two seeds in each block when planting tomatoes or lettuce. If both germinate, clip the weaker and smaller of the two off when it is about 2 weeks old. I do **not** recommend that the extra one be pulled out, as this may damage the root system of the other. It is only necessary to keep this kind of block moist for the first 10 days to two weeks. Use water without adding any nutrient. When the seedling is about 1 inch in height, it should be sprinkled once or twice daily with a half-strength nutrient solution.

To avoid damp-off and Pyrthium (or what is known as collar or stem rot), when the seedlings are well out of the block, mist them with a fine spray containing a 50-50 mix of Captan and Terraclor. Captan alone will do a good job but a

Tomato seedlings are ready to plant in growing beds when they are about 6 to 8 inches high.

Captan-Terraclor combination is better. The seedlings should be misted with this mix at least once a week. Particular care should be given to the stems just above the top of the block. It is at this point that this type of organism attacks the seedlings. This procedure should be followed for at least two weeks after the seedlings have been transplanted. When the seedling is small, the entire plant can be misted. As soon as it is sufficient size (1/16 inch in stem diameter), only the stems should be misted at the top of the block.

At the time it is ready to go into the growing beds, a good tomato seedling should be 6 to 8 inches tall and 6 to 8 inches broad, with a good heavy stem and root system (see photo). This means that the seedling blocks will have to be spread apart as the plants develop. Each seedling should have at least a 6 x 6-inch square growing space. They can be started in a much smaller area, but as they begin to develop, they must be moved apart. Otherwise they will become crowded and will begin to elongate and become thin and spindly. As they grow, the strength of the solution being fed to them each day should gradually be increased until it reaches the same concentration the plants will be fed when transplanted into the beds. It is also very important that they receive an adequate amount of sunlight. Lack of light will cause them to become too tall with correspondingly thin stems and sparse foliage. Their growth will also be soft and limp

Seedlings can be grown in this manner in the growing beds, but as a rule you should have a mature crop in the beds. When the old crop is taken out, having strong, well-developed seedlings ready to go back in will shorten the gap between planting and picking. The better the seedlings, the shorter the gap. It usually takes five to six weeks from the planting of the seed to grow a good seedling.

Once the seedling is started and at about the time the first true leaves appear above the cotyledons or seed leaves, the block containing the seedling should be placed in a tray or box containing either gravel or coarse sand. This box should have adequate drainage. When the seedlings are irrigated, the solution should drain out of the tray completely. With sand the plants will need less irrigation than with gravel. In either of these media, it usually takes at least two irrigations a day and sometimes three or four, depending on sunlight and temperatures.

I strongly recommend that you obtain a copy of the book *Greenhouse Tomatoes*, by Wittwer & Honma (see suppliers list). In my opinion it is the best possible guide for growing a good seedling. It has a very important section on temperatures used to give the tomato seedling what is called the "cold treatment." If you follow the directions given in this fine book and provide proper nutrition, you will have no trouble producing good seedlings.

After the greenhouse and medium have been properly sterilized and readied for planting, you are ready to set out your seedlings. If using gravel culture, the beds should be flooded to the overflow point. Close the fill and overflow pipes with cork stoppers and cut off the pumps. Holes should be scooped out in the gravel, spaced as shown in figure 23 deep enough so that there is ½ to 1 inch of solution standing in the holes. Holding the seedling by the

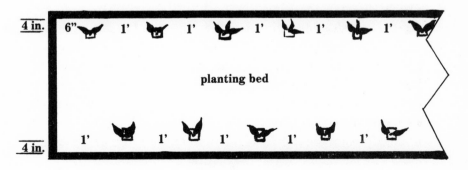

FIGURE 23.
Seedling Planting Diagram

block set it in the hole and pull the gravel around the block until it is level with the top. **Do not** bring the excess gravel up around the stem of the seedling. As soon as the bed is planted, remove the stopper so that the solution can drain back into the tank.

Plant tomato seedlings as shown in figure 23, with 1-foot spacing. Stagger them as shown, set in 4 inches from the sides. For cucumbers use 2-foot spacing, set 6 inches in from the sides. For lettuce and strawberries, allow each plant an area 6 inches square.

Tying and Suckering Plants

After the plant becomes well rooted and growth is progressing normally (usually two to three weeks), the remaining gravel can be pulled into place around the plant, leaving a completely level surface, with the block covered. At this point the plant should be sufficiently developed for you to start tying up the plants. Stretch heavy wire to each end of the unit, directly above the beds, about 6 inches from the roof. Attach nylon string to the base or lower stem of the plant. Fasten the other end of the string to the wire above the plant. Carefully clip plants to the nylon string (see photo). Paper-covered twist-ties can be used instead of plastic clips. Firmly attach the ties to the string before typing them to the plant.

You then should begin to sucker the plants (see next two photos). By grasping the sucker or lateral shoots between your thumb and finger and moving it in one direction and then another, the sucker should snap out. Some growers prefer to clip these suckers off with small shears. Be careful not to terminate the plant.

Pollinating

When the first buds begin to open on the tomato plants, you should begin to pollinate the flowers. In an open field,

94

Carefully clip the plant to the string using paper clips.

Suckering the tomato plant.

tomato plants are pollinated by wind movement. One very important factor to remember in achieving good pollination is that temperatures and humidity must be at the correct levels. If temperatures in the greenhouse drop too low, pollination will be very poor and the pollen may even become sterile. If the humidity is too low, the pollen will be too dry and will not adhere to the stigma. If the humidity is too high, the pollen will not shed readily, the pollen grains will stick together, and pollination will be poor or nonexistent.

Conditions are optimum for pollination when the temperature ranges from 68°F to 72°F and the humidity is the same level—68 to 72 percent. Good fruit sets can be obtained with the temperature between 65°F and 85°F and humidity ranging from 60 percent and 75 percent. For results these ranges should be at the bloom level, or level at which the last blossoms opened.

Near the floor of the greenhouse, the humidity will be higher and the temperature lower. Four feet from the floor there will be a considerable difference in both temperature and humidity. In a properly constructed greenhouse with good temperature control and air movement, if you use correct operating procedures, these temperatures and humidity levels will fall within the desired ranges most of the time.

Improper or poor pollination will result in less fruit set and much misshapen fruit. If the environment within the greenhouse is right, vibration of the blossoms will cause the pollen to shed freely and a good fruit set can be obtained. For best results the plants should be pollinated daily. It is possible to get a fairly good set by vibrating the plant every two or three days. The pollen is viable for three days. Theoretically in a good environment, a grower can achieve good fruit set by pollinating on that schedule. Unfortunately, however, this theory is not often borne out in actual practice. The grower who pollinates each day will achieve better production and better quality fruit than the one who does not.

Probably the least expensive and most readily available tool to use for good pollination, particularly for the grower with a small unit, is the rechargeable battery type electric tooth brush. This will usually operate for about an hour without having to be recharged. The brush should be taped thoroughly so that the user will not bruise or injure the stems. One touch of this vibrator to a cluster of blossoms is all that is necessary if conditions are conducive to pollination.

Once the plants have been strung up and the strings are taut, many growers simply walk through the building tapping the overhead wires supporting the plants. This is much faster than using a vibrator on each individual cluster. This system works well but will work even better if the grower uses a vibrator every third day and the tapping method on the other two.

There are a number of types of air blowers that work. A small vacuum cleaner with the air flow reversed or even a small hand-held electric hair dryer may be used. Many commercial growers use the large back-pack type mist blowers. Since they are gasoline driven, my biggest objection to these is that some damage may occur to the plants from unburned elements such as the hydrocarbons discharged into the greenhouse from the gasoline motors.

Pruning Excess Fruit and Foliage

As the fruit begins to form and set on the vines, if you have done a good job of pollination, you will usually note that each cluster contains from five to eight tomatoes. Some clusters may have more. If you wish to produce a large, well-shaped tomato, you should inspect the clusters for deformed and misshapen fruit as well as an excessive number of fruit. Although you may not want to, the misshapen and excess fruit should be pinched off. You should maintain five or six tomatoes on the first three or four clusters and

Remove foliage up to the first cluster of tomatoes.

four or five on the remainder. You will not only have better quality and shape in your fruit but will harvest more pounds per plant.

When the first cluster on the vine nears the ripening stage, you should remove the foliage below this cluster (see photo). These leaves contribute little to the growth and health of the plant, and removing them will give more light and air movement at the ground level, which will help in controlling fungus diseases. These branches can be easily removed by grasping them near the trunk of the plant and bending them up and down sharply. They should snap out, leaving a small lesion that will heal quickly. If shears are used, cut the branch off as close to the trunk as possible.

As the clusters begin to ripen higher up on the plant, this same procedure may be followed, but the upper portion of the plant should have a minimum of four feet of foliage at all times.

Terminating and Removing Plants

When the crop is nearing the end, the terminal stem in the top should be snapped or clipped off (see photo). This should be done about 50 days before you plan to pull the crop, which will give the last cluster in the top of the plant time to ripen following pollination. With no further plant

Snap off the terminal stem when the crop nears the end of its growing cycle.

growth, the last clusters will have larger fruit of better quality since all of the nutrient uptake will be diverted to this fruit.

To remove the plants, first cut the stem about six inches above the growing medium and remove the upper parts of the plants from the greenhouse. Pump the beds full and stop up the fill and overflow pipes with corks, allowing the beds to remain full of solution. While you grasp the stump of the plant firmly and pull it up, use a side-to-side shaking movement. This will allow most of the root system to pull free of the medium. Shake out any gravel remaining in the roots. Remove the plants from the greenhouse and burn them if possible.

Cucumbers

The same general procedures used in starting tomato seedlings should be used when starting cucumber plants, but only one seed should be used per block. The seed should be placed in the block with the sharp pointed end down. If this is not done, when the seed germinates, the plant will grow downward. It will then have to curl to come back up out of the block. Since the hole is rather small, the seedling will often become so curled and misshapen that it is of no value.

Cucumbers grow to the seedling stage much more rapidly than tomatoes. In three weeks the seedlings should be ready to go into the growing beds. More space is needed per plant because of the heavy foliage, however. Best results will be obtained if planting is done as shown in figure 23. In various tests I have found that in a commercial unit designed to contain 1100 tomato plants, I had space for 600 cucumber plants. I have gotten a much higher total yield in pounds of good fruit from 600 well-spaced plants than I could by growing 800 to 1000 plants in the same unit. Cucumber seedlings should be treated with the Captan-Terraclor mix just as the tomato seedlings were.

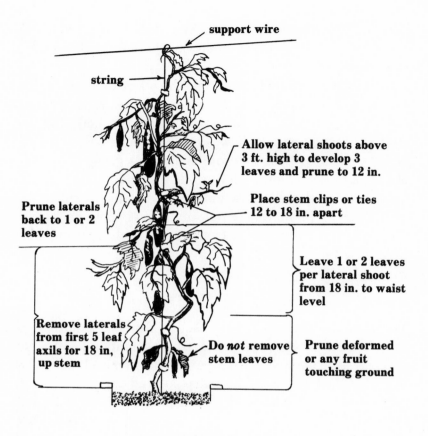

support wire

string

Allow lateral shoots above 3 ft. high to develop 3 leaves and prune to 12 in.

Place stem clips or ties 12 to 18 in. apart

Prune laterals back to 1 or 2 leaves

Leave 1 or 2 leaves per lateral shoot from 18 in. to waist level

Remove laterals from first 5 leaf axils for 18 in, up stem

Do *not* remove stem leaves

Prune deformed or any fruit touching ground

FIGURE 24.
Cucumber Pruning Diagram

As soon as the plants are well rooted in the growing beds, they will need to be strung up like tomato plants. The cucumber is an extremely fast-growing plant and when cared for and fed properly is a very heavy producer. Only the seedless varieties should be used. Varieties highly recommended for excellent production include Tosca 70, Rocket, Fertila, Burpless, and the Fem varieties, such as Femdan, Femfrance, etc. (see suppliers list).

All these varieties have no male blossoms and are self-pollinating. Each blossom should produce one cucumber. If

102

Remove all curled or misshapen cucumbers like the one shown here.

you notice any male blossoms (growing directly out of the axil), they should be picked immediately to avoid pollination, as they will cause fruit to be misshapen (see photo). The plants should be trimmed as shown in figure 24. You will also note that a number of the fruits will abort. This is a built-in characteristic of these varieties. When the plant puts out an excessive number of fruits, some of them will not develop. If the fruit begins to curl excessively and yellow, this indicates that the plant is not receiving enough nitrogen.

The cucumber plant is a very heavy feeder, and it is almost impossible to overfeed or overwater it. If the temperature and humidity are being controlled as recommended for tomato growth, the cucumbers will not produce as heavily as they should. Where only cucumbers are grown, nutrient strength should be doubled since cucumbers need twice the average amount of nutrient fed to tomatoes. If you are mixing your own nutrient, the nitrogen content of this nutrient should be doubled. Temperatures should be kept considerably higher. A minimum of 70°F should be maintained and a high humidity level is beneficial. With these higher temperatures and humidity levels, however, mildew is almost certain to occur unless preventive steps are taken, as discussed in chapter 5.

Lettuce

Lettuce seed should be planted exactly as tomato seed, and the seedlings should be transplanted into the beds in three to four weeks. There are many varieties of lettuce, and it is one of the easiest vegetables to grow. There are a number of new varieties, such as the Chessibb and Ostinata (see suppliers list), that mature very rapidly and are delicious. Seedlings should be set in the growing beds using the same procedure as for other plants. It is necessary to allow a space 6 x 6 inches for each plant.

Lettuce will thrive under the same environmental conditions as tomatoes, but it can be grown at far lower temperatures. In fact, for optimum production lower temperatures are recommended. For commercial growers this means a large saving in fuel costs in the winter months. The best temperature for growing lettuce is 50°F, but it is possible to grow a good lettuce crop at 40°F. The only effect this will have is to slow the growth to some extent. The area of the greenhouse most likely to be shaded or with the least light can also be utilized for lettuce.

The Ostinata variety will tolerate more heat than most varieties. By shading the greenhouse in the summer and setting the thermostat controlling the cooling system to actuate fans when temperatures reach 60°F, I have been able to produce excellent lettuce throughout the summer months with outside temperatures ranging from 90° to 110°F. Most lettuce varieties bolt or go to seed in hotter weather, but if proper care and attention are given to temperature and shading, a number of varieties can be successfully grown in the warmer months.

The growing blocks should be left on the lettuce when it is harvested. When the head, with block intact, is placed in a cellophane bag, it may be refrigerated. This will keep the lettuce crisp and fresh until it is served.

Other Varieties

Almost any vegetable can be grown in hydroponic units (see color plates). Sweet corn is very prolific. The seed can be planted in the gravel just as it would be in soil. Be careful to place corn seeds deep enough in the gravel so that the solution will reach them during the pumping cycle. I have had excellent success planting corn in this manner. Allow 6-inch spacing. Beside each grain of corn, plant one bean, such as the Blue Lake or Kentucky Wonder. As they emerge, the vines will climb the corn stalks. By the time

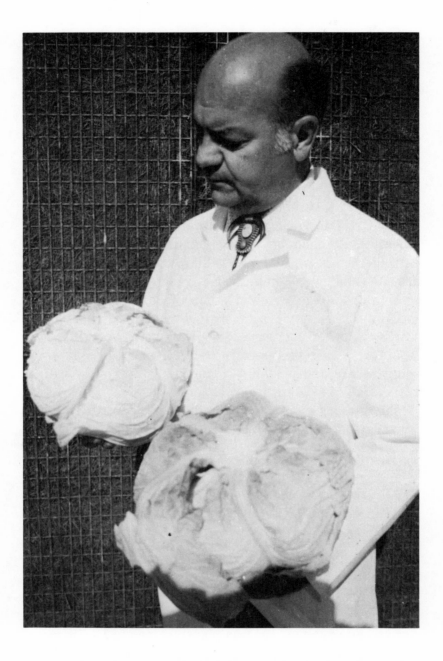

John R. Myers, director of research, Hydroculture, Inc., holds two giant hydroponically grown cabbages.

the corn is ready to be harvested, the beans should also be ready.

Radishes, shallots, and onions can be grown underneath tomato plants. They should be planted along the edges of the beds so they will not be completely shaded by the larger plant. Some types of lettuce and chard will also do well as an "under" crop. You can sow the seeds or plant the sets just as you would in soil. Eggplant and peppers should be grown following the same procedure as tomatoes. Do not attempt to grow any of the hot varieties of pepper in the same unit with sweet pepper, however. If you do, you will most likely end up with all hot pepper.

Strawberries are another crop that will produce well when grown in a hydroponic system with a controlled environment. The ever-bearing varieties are recommended. Temperature and humidity ranges are the same as those recommended for tomatoes, and nutritional needs are virtually the same as well, although occasional deficiencies in iron and nitrogen may occur. The principal problem in growing strawberries is that they need far less water than most plants. Overwatering will result in little or no production. For this reason it is recommended that they be grown in a separate bed. There are small units available for the home that have been used with good results (see suppliers list). One pumping cycle daily will usually be sufficient, but two or more may be needed in the summer months. The use of a small blower once a day when the plants are flowering will help fruit setting and development.

Cabbage (see photo) and melons (see color plates) are also excellent crops.

Flowers

For the flower grower, the ornamental varieties of pepper plants make a beautiful addition to other flowers in the beds. Almost any flower plant can be grown as well, if not better, through hydroponics as in conventional floral culture (see color plates). Among those I have grown with excellent results are gladiolus, tulips, amaryllis, all types of ivy, roses, and carnations. In growing gladiolus, tulips, and other bulbs, the corms can be planted side by side with 1 inch or less separating them. They should be placed in the growing medium so that the bottom of the corm (and be sure you place them in with the *bottom down*) just reaches the solution level when the beds are irrigated. Almost any other type of flower can and has been grown hydroponically with excellent results.

Cuttings will root very quickly in blocks, but there are also rooting stimulators available that accelerate root growth. These are especially good for hard-to-propagate species (see suppliers list). Most people will want to grow a number of varieties, both vegetable and flower, in the same unit. This can certainly be done. Results will be satisfactory for most growers if a median is established for all of the factors.

When to Plant

Spring crops of tomatoes yield best when planted in January in the southern half of the nation and February or early March in northern states.

For fall crops in almost all areas, July and August plantings are recommended. In the northern areas, it is necessary to get the fall crop in as early as possible. This will allow a good crop-set on the vines before the onset of low light intensity and cold temperatures.

In areas where the winters are severe with a corresponding short growing season, many growers have gone to a one-crop cycle for tomatoes. By planting in late February or early March, the crop can be carried to October or later. The system is then planted with lettuce or other crops that do well at lower light intensities and temperatures. This also affords the grower a considerable saving in heating costs.

Since cucumbers are heat-loving plants, they should be planted in late spring and taken out in early fall, except in areas where the outside temperatures seldom fall below 40°F.

By studying a plant's needs and growth patterns, planting schedules for different species can be worked out in order to reap the maximum harvest.

Miscellaneous Tips

One point I would like to emphasize is that with *all* growing there is no substitute for "tender loving care." To produce a good crop of any kind successfully, you must have the proper equipment and follow correct operating procedures. Using the one asset that all of us have—common sense— there is no reason why one cannot be successful.

Most growers like to keep records of planting dates and weight of fruit. This adds much to a grower's knowledge and pleasure.

Between crops and before replanting, in addition to sterilizing the growing medium, you should wash the walls, shelves, and walkways with a strong chlorine solution. Use a spray or smoke-type pesticide and fungicide to fumigate the house.

Wash all clips, brushes, pump, and tools in a mixture half Clorox and half water; then rinse them in clean water and let them dry for 24 hours.

If you plan on taking an extended vacation and do not have someone you can depend on to care for your greenhouse, you should clean out the old crops and "lay the house by."

If properly built, the house and system will continue to function with little care. You must remember, however,

Commercial hydroponic "Magic Garden" growing unit is 26 ft. wide x 128 ft. long.

that problems usually develop faster in a controlled environment than outside. Plant growth is accelerated and crops need to be harvested more frequently.

Where possible, the installation of shelves is recommended. They may be used for potted plants and tools. A small cabinet is also useful for storing supplies. Nutrient and the pH tester should be stored out of direct sunlight and in a dry, cool place.

Two other fixtures that can be installed in the greenhouse and that you will find very useful are a hose bibb on the water supply line and a small wash basin.

Some useful tools are a toilet brush and sponges for cleaning the sump, a toothbrush for cleaning the pumps, a minimum-maximum thermometer (hang near cooling thermostats), a small garden hose, a stiff broom, rubber or plastic gloves, a pair of small pruning shears, a sharp knife, pliers, and a small crescent wrench. Sumps and pumps should be cleaned each time the solution is changed.

The floor area not utilized for beds and equipment can be beautified by covering with Astro Turf or indoor-outdoor carpeting. For units not having concrete floors, floors made of 1 x 4-inch slats with ½-inch interstices may be desired.

Have the telephone number of a good electrician available, as the crop can be damaged or lost in very short time from extreme heat or cold if a breakdown occurs.

Check the water level and adjust the pH daily.

Keep acid, pesticides, and fungicides locked up out of reach of small children.

Plant Disease
and Insect Problems

DISEASES

In this chapter I will deal only with the more common
diseases and pests you might encounter. If you find your
plants infected with a disease or insect you cannot identify
or control, you should contact your county agent or an
agricultural college or university. I would highly recommend that all growers, whether hobbyist or commercial
operator, write to the various universities for lists of any
bulletins that may be available.

Among those whose bulletins and booklets I have found
extremely helpful are Ohio State University, Texas A&M
University, Rutgers University, New York State College
of Agricultural and Life Sciences (Cornell University), and
Michigan State University (see suppliers list). There are
many others that may be helpful.

All recommended fungicides and insecticides are listed at
the end of this chapter.

Fungus

Probably the most common plant diseases are the various
types of fungi such as the leaf molds and mildews. If you

111

have a greenhouse with a completely controlled environment, the best way to prevent these fungus-type diseases is warm temperature, low humidity, and proper air circulation. If you run into a long period of cold, cloudy, humid weather and allow your temperatures to remain near minimum levels with high humidity, you are most certainly going to find your plants suffering from some type of fungus.

In tomatoes the most common fungi are the *leaf molds*. These can usually be identified by small patches of spores on the leaves themselves. These grayish spots appear on the older leaves first. Velvety green or brownish spots will appear on the underside of the leaf. Once these begin to form, any movement of the plant will send thousands of the spores into the air and these fungi will spread throughout the greenhouse very rapidly. They can be controlled by using one or more of the recommended fungicides listed at the end of this chapter. Always use them according to the manufacturer's directions.

The worst fungus found in tomato plants is *Botrytis*. This is a gray mold that not only forms around the base of the stem and destroys it, but also attacks the fruit around the calyx, causing it to rot in a few hours. This mold progresses through the plants very quickly and once it gets established in a greenhouse, it can destroy an entire crop. A cold and wet environment provides the perfect setting for Botrytis. I have been able to bring it under control through the use of high temperatures and by making the humidity as low as possible. Botrytis spores apparently will not live in a hot, dry environment.

The old treatments such as Bordeaux paste are time consuming to use and not completely effective. Botran and Bravo are effective if treatment is started early enough. Termil has recently been approved in some areas and is very effective on almost all of the fungus diseases including Botrytis. Before using any fungicide or pesticide, however, you should check to see if its use is approved both in your state and by the USDA. From time to time, new pesticides and fungicides are released while others are banned. Always check the manufacturer's recommendations carefully, especially those regarding limitations on fruit harvest. Fungicidal and pesticidal smokes are also available as shown in the list at the end of this chapter.

Fungus, particularly "downy mildew," is the most common problem in cucumbers. Because the desirable temperatures and humidity levels for growing cucumbers are conducive to mildew growth, a preventive spray program is recommended to counteract the mildew. Any approved mildew fungicide spray may be used. Again, good cultural and sanitation practices are a must.

Potato Virus

Another fairly common disease of tomatoes is potato virus. This is also identified as double-streak virus. I once saw a number of tomato crops badly infected by this virus. The seedlings for these crops were grown by a supplier who used, as a potting mix, soil in which potatoes had previously been grown. This resulted in a very large loss of fruit. Usually the first symptoms noted are elongated brown streaks on the stem of the plant. These may extend out into the branches and even the leaves. The fruit will be pitted and splotched and will look as if the tomatoes were infected with smallpox or measles. If the fruit is peeled, there will be no evidence of the virus inside the tomato itself. This virus can spread throughout a crop rather rapidly, and there are no known sprays that are effective against it. I have seen one or two occurrences of potato virus where it seemingly died out of its own accord. One operator thought this was due to his use of Maneb as a fungicide.

Potatoes can be very easily grown hydroponically, but under no circumstances should you attempt to grow potatoes and tomatoes in the same system or the same green-house. Nor should you follow a potato crop with a tomato crop unless the house and the growing beds have been thoroughly sterilized. There are several sterilizers that will kill potato virus, such as methyl bromide, but these are dangerous to use and are not recommended unless it becomes absolutely necessary. The best remedy is simply not to grow potatoes if you are a tomato grower.

Tomato Mosaics

Another tomato disease that has been given much notoriety over the years is commonly called *tobacco mosaic*. It is recommended that a grower **not** smoke or carry tobacco into a greenhouse where tomatoes are being grown. Most authorities recommend that the worker who uses tobacco wash his hands in a good disinfectant or detergent before handling the plants. This is good sanitation.

Dr. Merle Jensen of the Environmental Laboratory at Tucson, Arizona, is one of the world's leading authorities on greenhouse culture. He once said that it was his belief that mosaic in tomato plants was a separate and distinct virus strain. I tend to agree with him. Mosaic symptoms seem to occur in a greenhouse where light conditions are not good and where the temperatures are too cool, particularly in shaded areas. I have visited hundreds of greenhouse tomato operations over the past 14 years, and I have yet to see one that did not have some plants showing symptoms of this virus. It is known that there are several different strains, and depending on the type, the symptoms may include mottling, a grayish cast, and stringy leaves.

I have seen other tomato crops that the operators were sure were infected with a mosaic. In one case, after careful examination and investigation, I discovered the "mosaic" was caused by outside herbicides used near the windward side of the greenhouse, and pulled into the building by the cooling system. The leaf and growth patterns were very similar to those of the mosaics.

As another example, an operator of a hydroponic unit in California asked me to visit his installation to see if I could determine what his problem was. A change in his plants, which were approximately 6 feet tall, had taken place at about the 4-foot level. If you stood at one end of the house and looked down the rows and had drawn a string the length of the building at the 4-foot level, you could see that every plant had the same wild growth from that point upward. On investigation it was found that at an airport over a mile away, crop dusters using an herbicide had been refilling their tanks, the wind had carried this herbicide to the greenhouse area, where it was dispersed throughout the building by the cooling system. One oddity of this particular occurrence was that there did not seem to be a great deal of loss in the amount of fruit set, although the fruit itself had undergone a distinct change in conformation. All of the fruit on or above this 4-foot line looked like the old Oxheart variety of tomato with the sides flattened and the blossom ends very pointed.

Since most authorities believe that the mosaic virus is likely to be spread through a crop by workers handling the infected plants, it is common practice to remove any plants showing decided mosaic symptoms. I once left 30 plants, all of which were infected with mosaic, in a unit containing 1100 plants. The symptoms became very marked at about the time the plants were setting the third and fourth clusters of fruit. For the duration of the crop, there was no further spread of the disease, but there was some drop in production of the afflicted plants as compared to the rest of the crop.

Most varieties used today are resistant to mosaic. If you use these resistant varieties and employ good sanitation and cultivating practices, your plants will overcome the disease with little or no loss of production, although they may show some symptoms. Above all, you should see that the plants are fed a properly balanced diet. Just as a human is weakened through malnutrition and becomes more susceptible to disease, the same holds true for plants.

The varieties of seeds included on the suppliers list are recommended because they show resistance to mosaic and many other diseases common to the tomato. The Ohio State University has been very helpful to tomato growers in developing mosaic-resistant varieties.

In recent years there has been much work done inoculating seedlings with tomato mosaic virus. This research shows much promise for the eventual elimination of the problem.

I have grown crop after crop of lettuce with no disease problems whatsoever. Occasionally Botrytis can be a problem. In all of these crops, whether grown by the hobbyist or the commercial grower, the various bulletins mentioned earlier, published by the different universities, will be of great value in diagnosing the problem and finding a cure.

INSECTS

The insects most likely to be encountered in greenhouse growing are spider mites, white fly, pinworms, cut worms, and aphids.

Spider Mites

The spider mites, and there are several different families of these, will spread very rapidly through a crop once they get a foothold. Fortunately there are a number of sprays and smokes that can be used to eliminate them. If your crop is attacked by spider mites, you will first notice leaves beginning to turn pale and yellow. Spider mites feed by sucking the juices from the leaves. Although they are virtually microscopic in size, their presence can be determined by looking on the underside of the leaf. As the mites begin to spread, very fine webs will be noticed on the plants.

Normally three applications of the right pesticide (see the end of this chapter) will take care of them, used on a two- or three-day schedule. This will kill the adults and at the same time break the hatching cycle. If not stopped, spiker mites will very rapidly defoliate a tomato or cucumber crop.

White Fly

The white fly is probably the most common pest found in the world today, particularly in greenhouse tomato production. White flies seem to thrive in all parts of the world and will build up a resistance to any pesticide very rapidly. Only by extreme care can they be controlled. I have often thought that if anyone ever built a greenhouse at the North Pole in which to grow tomatoes, sooner or later it would be infested with white flies. I have listed a number of pesticides that are used for white fly control. You should vary what you apply to avoid having these pests become immune. I believe that the best hope for controlling these insects will eventually be through biological means. A new control for white fly, Prescription Treatment #1200 containing Resmethrin (SBP 1382) is being reported as very effective by growers who have used it (see suppliers list).

Pinworm

The pinworm is another very destructive insect and can completely destroy a tomato crop. This pest is probably the hardest of all to eliminate. The pinworm, like other members of the worm family, comes from a moth egg. The moths lay eggs in the tops of the plants. When the eggs hatch, the worm develops between the leaf tissues. Pinworm may also be found under the calyx on tomatoes, in

117

the stems of the plant, and where two tomatoes make contact in a cluster. There are a number of reasons why they are extremely hard to control. They have a very long incubation cycle, and since the worm spends its lifetime inside the leaf or some other part of the plant, the normal pesticides will not reach it.

When this worm reaches maturity, it emerges from its hiding place and drops to the ground. In the case of hydroponic culture, it burrows into the growing medium and later emerges as a moth to start the life cycle anew. There are numerous pesticides available that will kill the moth, but if one or more live long enough to deposit their eggs on the plant, it becomes virtually impossible to control them through the use of any spray or other form of pesticide. As with the white fly, there have been some very promising developments in biological control of this pest in recent years.

Most of the other worms that create problems for growers, such as the cutworm and a number of its cousins, can be controlled by the use of pesticides.

Aphids

Aphids as a rule do not create any problem for tomato growers, but they can and do attack cucumbers, melons, and most all of the floral crops. They are especially destructive to pepper plants. I have yet to grow peppers that sooner or later did not become infested with aphids— usually sooner!

The pyrethrum sprays have been very effective in controlling these pests and helping to control numerous others. Since these sprays are considered nonresidual, as are some of the smokes and fogs used as pesticides, they are much preferred over many of the other sprays.

Biological Control

Mr. Richard Myers, former research director for Hydroculture, Inc., Glendale, Arizona, has made tremendous prog-

118

ress in the biological control of both the pinworm and the white fly. In controlled tests he used four small Button Quail per building housing 1100 tomato plants. The pinworms in these units were kept at a bare minimum. He has also used a number of other small birds with like results. These birds do not feed on the fruit or damage the plant in any manner. In the units in which he used these quail, an occasional moth might be seen, but there was no damage during the entire crop cycle. The control units using standard pesticide procedures were heavily damaged by the worms, with much loss of fruit, and there were other adverse effects from the sprays as well.

After a long and arduous search, Mr. Richard Oxford, former head of biological control for Hydroculture, Inc., was able to identify a very tiny, almost microscopic wasp for use in control of the white fly. The results of his work in this area are very promising.

Another enemy of the white fly that Mr. Myers has used with considerable success, is the chameleon. These small members of the lizard family are voracious insect eaters. The use of them, however, had a somewhat comic side effect. Researchers found that one of these harmless little fellows dropping down a collar or running up a leg would cause a stampede among their workers that resulted in more damage to a crop than the white fly!

Much work is also being done in this area by other researchers. Hopefully, in the near future we may see complete control of all the destructive pests through the use of their natural enemies.

Biodegradable Spray

One method of controlling white flies that has been used with a great deal of success by many growers is the use of a biodegradable detergent as a spray. There are several of these on the market, and numerous growers report excellent results with their use (see suppliers list). Normal solution is 2 tablespoons to 1 gallon of water, and it can be sprayed once or twice a week. When using any of the various sprays, care should be taken to follow the manufacturer's directions. Also, the finer the mist, the better the control of the insects.

Nematodes

Nematodes are another problem occasionally seen in hydroponics but are not as prevalent as in soil culture. They are microscopic worms that attack the roots, forming large nodes, and can be carried into the unit in mud on the feet of the workers. They also may be picked up if you are careless when putting gravel into the growing beds. They can be eliminated by sterilizing the beds with one of the several nematicides listed. I have had excellent results with Nemagon, used as follows: mix emulsified Nemagon at the rate of 1 quart per 100 gallons of water. Mix it in the sump and pump it into the beds and let it stand overnight. While pumping the solution out, flush the beds from the top with fresh water to wash thoroughly. Wash the sump walls down before refilling.

Other Insect Controls

Some growers have found it helpful in controlling insects to plant marigolds, basil, or garlic near the base of the plants. These plants could also be planted outside, around the perimeter of the greenhouse. One or more of these plants will help to repel many bothersome insects.

Various species of insects are attracted to either the ultraviolet colors or colors such as yellow. If one or more of either of these types of lights are used, some method of destroying the insects must be devised. Possible methods involve positioning a small container of water and oil directly below the light or hanging fly strips in close proximity to the lights. Some success has even been achieved by lightly coating the lights with grease. There are also low-voltage electric "Bug Killers" on the market that will attract and electrocute some insects.

DISEASES, INSECTS, AND THEIR CONTROL

Diseases	Fungicides
Damp-off Pythium	Fulex ADO
Botrytis	Botran
	Bravo
	Exotherm-Termil
Leaf Molds	Maneb
	Manzate
	Dithane 22

Insects	Insecticides
White fly	Fulex DI-THIO (if approved)
	Resmethrin
Pinworms, white fly, loopers, climbing cut worms, spider mites	Thiodan
	Dibrom
	Malathion
	Vapona (DDVP)
	Sevin
Aphids	Aphid Smoke
	Malathion

Order bulletins from one of the universities for additional information or news of new controls.

Reference Material and Suppliers List

REFERENCE MATERIAL

Some of the listed books are out of print, but they may be found in local libraries. Many book dealers have sources for locating out-of-print books.

BOOKS

Gardening Without a Garden
Dr. E. Saub
525 N. Colgate Ave.
Anaheim, CA 92801

Greenhouse Tomatoes, Guidelines for Successful Production
S. H. Wittwer and S. Honma
Michigan State University Press
East Lansing, MI 48823

Guide To Commercial Hydroponics
M. Schwarz
Israel Universities Press
New York, London, Jerusalem
Kiryat Moshe, P. O. Box 7145
Jerusalem, Israel

How To Build a Solar Heater
Ted Lucas
Ward Ritchie Press
474 S. Arroyo Pkwy.
Pasadena, CA 91105

Hunger Signs in Crops
H. B. Sprague
David McKay Co.
New York, NY 10017

Hydroponics, The Gardening Without Soil
Dudley Harris
Purnell and Sons (S.A.) (Pty.), Ltd.
70 Keerom St.
Cape Town, South Africa

Profitable Growing Without Soil
H. F. Hollis
English Universities Press Ltd.
102 Newgard St.
London, EGL

Soilless Growth of Plants
(Out of print)
Carleton Ellis and M. W. Swaney,
Revised by Tom Eastwood
Reinhold Publishing Corp.
New York, NY

Successful Gardening Without Soil
C. E. Ticquet
Chemical Publishing Co., Inc.
155 W. 19th St.
New York, NY 10011

Your Homemade Greenhouse (And How To Build It)
Jack Kramer
Cornerstone Library Publications
Simon & Schuster
New York, NY

MAGAZINES

American Vegetable Grower
Willoughby, OH 44094

Better Homes and Gardens
1716 Locust St.
Des Moines, IA 50336

Farm Journal
230 W. Washington Sq.
Philadelphia, PA 19105

Flower and Garden
4251 Pennsylvania
Kansas City, MO 64111

Horticulture
Massachusetts Horticultural
Society
300 Massachusetts Ave.
Boston, MA 02115

Plants Alive
Dept. H-11, 2100 N. 45th St.
Seattle, WA 98103

Progressive Farmer
820 Shades Creek Pkwy.
Birmingham, AL 35202

Southern Living
P. O. Box 523
Birmingham, AL 35202

UNIVERSITIES

Most of all the universities that include any course relating to agriculture in their curriculum publish material I have found helpful. They have catalogs listing the material available and the cost of each publication. Among those whose publications have been of help to many growers, including myself are:

Extension Service
University of Florida
Gainesville, FL 32601

Cooperative Extension Service
University of Illinois
Urbana, IL 61801

Cooperative Extension Service
Louisiana State University
Baton Rouge, LA 70803

Department of Horticulture
University of Missouri
Columbia, MO 65201

The Cooperative Extension
Service
Ohio State University
Columbus, OH 43210

Soil Testing Laboratory
Purdue University
Agronomy Dept.
Lafayette, IN 47907

SUPPLIERS

Many of the items needed for building your own greenhouse or setting up your own hydroponic system can be obtained locally or in a large city close by. I have tried to list sources throughout the United States. I am sure there are many others I am not familiar with.

AEROSOL SPRAYS

B & G Co.
2419 South Blvd.
Houston, TX 77006

Big State Chemical
2822 Leeland
Houston, TX 77003

DAO Corporation
Box 659
Terre Haute, IN 47808

Virginia Chemicals, Inc.
Portsmouth, VA 23703

Whitmire Laboratories
  (Resmethrin)
3568 Tree Court Industrial Blvd.
St. Louis, MO 63122

ALARM SYSTEMS — TEMPERATURE

E. C. Geiger
Box 2853
Harleysville, PA 19438

Meskers, Inc.
634 River Vale Rd.
Rivervale, NJ 07675

ARTIFICIAL LIGHTING FOR PLANTS

Growers Supply Co.
Dept. 1132-H
Ann Arbor, MI 48103

Sylvania Lighting Products
60 Boston St.
Salem, MA 10970

Local electrical fixture dealers

ASPARAGUS CROWNS

Dean Foster Nursery
Hartford, MI 49057

ASPEN FIBER COOLING PADS

Western Aspen Division
American Excelsior Corp.
900 Ave. H East
Arlington, TX 76010

Western Wood Division
American Excelsior Corp.
8320 Canford St.
Pico Rivera, CA 90660

BLOCKS — PLANTING

BR8 Gro Blocks — Famco
300 Lake Rd.
Medina, OH 44256.

Kys Cubes
American Plant Container Co.
2600 Wisconsin Ave.
Downers Grove, IL 60515

Keyes Fibre Co.
Box 806
New Iberia, LA 70560

2 J's and 1 D of Houston
7202 Brownwood
Houston, TX 77020

Plant Products Co., Ltd.
314 Orenda
Bramalea, Ontario
Canada

*Most greenhouse supply
  companies*

BULBS

Davids & Royston Bulb Co.
1577 W. 132nd St.
Gardena, CA 90240

Jednak Floral Co.
P. O. Box 1917
Columbus, OH 43216

John Scheepers, Inc.
63 Wall St.
New York, NY 10005

Van Bourgondiens
245 Farmingdale Rd.
Rt. 109, Box A
Babylon, NY 11702

CO$_2$ DISPENSERS

George Ball, Inc.
West Chicago, IL 60185
or
George Ball Pacific, Inc.
Box 10175
Palo Alto, CA 94303

*Most greenhouse supply
    companies*

COOLING & VENTILATION EQUIPMENT

Acme Engineering & Manufac-
    turing Corporation
Box 978
Muskogee, OK 77401

W. W. Grainger, Inc.
5959 W. Howard St.
Chicago, IL 60648
(Sales offices in most major cities)

Growers International
6352 Alder St.
Houston, TX 77036

Ickes-Braun Glasshouses
Box 147
Deerfield, IL 60015

Modine Manufacturing Co.
1500 Dekoven Ave.
Racine, WI 53401

Phil Rich Fan Company
(Windmaster)
7200 Old Katy Road
Houston, TX 77055

Texas Greenhouse Co., Inc.
2717 St. Louis Ave.
Fort Worth, TX 76110

Texfan, Inc.
15025 Main
Houston, TX 77001

Windmaker Fan Co.
1001 West Loop N.
Houston, TX 77005

Wolfe Wholesale Florist
P. O. Box 330
Waco, TX 76708

COOLERS — EVAPORATIVE

Most cities in the West and South
have local manufacturers of evaporative coolers. Since they are a
large and heavy item to ship, I
would suggest consulting local
manufacturers.

W. W. Grainger, Inc.
5959 W. Howard St.
Chicago, IL 60648
(Offices most cities)

Goettl Bros. Metal Products, Inc.
2005 East Indian School Rd.
Phoenix, AZ 80516

CONTAINERS FOR VEGETABLES (boxes)

Container Services, Inc.
2833 Hansboro
Dallas, TX 75233

Lone Star Corrugated Container
 Corp.
1266 Profit Dr.
Dallas, TX 75247

CORRUGATED CLOSURE STRIPS FOR FIBERGLASS PANELS

Filon Corporation
12333 S. Van Ness Ave.
Hawthorne, CA 90250

Closures, Inc.
P. O. Box 55392
Houston, TX 77005

FIBERGLASS PANELS

Filon Division,
Vistron Corporation
12333 S. Van Ness Ave.
Hawthorne, CA 90250

Growers International
6352 Alder St.
Houston, TX 77036

Ickes-Braun Glasshouses
Box 147
Deerfield, IL 60015

Lasco Industries, Inc.
1561 Chapin Rd.
Montebello, CA 90640

Ornyte-Berdoninc
711 Olympic Blvd.
Santa Monica, CA 90400

Poly-Growers, Inc.
Box 294
Muncy, PA 17756

Texas Greenhouse Co., Inc.
2717 St. Louis Ave.
Fort Worth, TX 76110

Wolfe Wholesale Florist
P. O. Box 330
Waco, TX 76708

FOGGERS

Aero-Dyne Manufacturing Corp.
3505 W. Main
Emmetsburg, LA 50536

Brighton By-Products Co., Inc.
P. O. Box 23
New Brighton, PA 15066

Carmel Chemical Corp.
P. O. Box 406
Westfield, IN 46074

E. C. Geiger
Box 285
Harleysville, PA 19438

Micro-Gen Corp.
8127 Vidor Dr.
San Antonio, TX 78216

Wolfe Wholesale Florist
Box 330
Waco, TX 76708

GREENHOUSE INSURANCE

Florists Mutual
500 St. Louis St.
Edwardsville, IL 62025

GREENHOUSES

Greenhouse Plans

Contact the agricultural extension service in your state for information on availability of plans
suitable for your area.

Small Greenhouses for the Home

Aquaponics
22135 Ventura Blvd.
Woodland Hills, CA 91365

Aluminum Greenhouses, Inc.
14615 Lorain Ave.
Cleveland, OH 44111

Gothic Arch Greenhouses
P. O. Box 1654
Mobile, AL 36601

Lord and Burnham
Irvington-on-Hudson
New York, NY 10533

G. H. McGregor Greenhouses
Box 36-35
Santa Cruz, CA 95063

Porta Green Co.
7600 Wall St.
Cleveland, OH 44125

Redwood Domes, Division SC
Aptos, CA 95003

Peter Reimuller Greenhouses
P. O. Box 2666
Santa Cruz, CA 95063

Texas Greenhouse Co., Inc.
2717 St. Louis Ave.
Fort Worth, TX 76110

Commercial Greenhouses

Environmental Structures
7600 Wall St.
Cleveland, OH 44125

Ickes-Braun Glasshouses
Box 147
Deerfield, IL 60015

Inclosures, Inc.
80 Main St.
Moreland, GA 30259

Lord and Burnham
Irvington-on-Hudson
New York, NY 10533

National Greenhouse Co.
Pana, IL 62557

Poly-Growers, Inc.
Box 294
Muncy, PA 17756

X. S. Smith, Inc.
Drawer X
Red Bank, NJ 07701

Texas Greenhouse Co., Inc.
2717 St. Louis Ave.
Fort Worth, TX 76110

Turner Green Houses
Rt. 117
South Goldsboro, NC 27530

Van Wingerden Plastic Greenhouse Co.
Horseshoe, NC 28742

GREENHOUSE SUPPLIES

These firms stock a wide range of
products for the greenhouse.

Aquaponics
22135 Ventura Blvd.
Woodland Hills, CA 91364

George J. Ball
West Chicago, IL 60185
or
George Ball Pacific, Inc.
Box 10175
Palo Alto, CA 94303

Brawley Seed Co., Inc.
Mooresville, NC 28115

Brighton By-Products Co., Inc.
Box 23
New Brighton, PA 15006

Cassco
Box 550
Montgomery, AL 36101

DAO Corporation
Box 659
Terre Haute, IN 47808

E. C. Geiger
Box 285
Harleysville, PA 19438

Georgia Golf & Garden Supply
Co., Inc.
100-D Piedmont Ct.
Doraville, GA 30340

Growers International
6352 Alder St.
Houston, TX 77036

Hydroponic Hobbies
302 Town & Country Village
Sunnyvale, CA 94086

Jacobs Bros.
8928 Sepulveda Blvd.
Sepulveda, CA 91343

Jednak Floral Co.
Box 1917
Columbus, OH 43216

Mellinger's Inc.
North Lima, OH 44452

Plant Products Co., Ltd.
314 Orenda
Bramalea, Ontario
Canada

Stuppy's
120 E. 12th Ave.
North Kansas City, MO 64116

Texas Greenhouse, Inc.
2717 St. Louis Ave.
Fort Worth, TX 76110

Wolfe Wholesale Florist
Box 330
Waco, TX 76708

Waterworks Gardenhouses
P. O. Box 2599
Castro Valley, CA 94546

HADITE

Domtar Ltd.
3065 Mavis
Mississagua, Ontario
Canada

Featherlite Corp.
Ranger, TX 76470

HEATING EQUIPMENT

W. W. Grainger, Inc.
5959 W. Howard St.
Chicago, IL 60648

Growers International
6352 Alder St.
Houston, TX 77036

Ickes-Braun Glasshouses
Box 147
Deerfield, IL 60015

Modine Manufacturing Co.
1500 Dekoven Ave.
Racine, WI 53401

Texas Greenhouse Co., Inc.
2717 St. Louis Ave.
Fort Worth, TX 76110

Wolfe Wholesale Florist
P. O. Box 330
Waco, TX 76708

HEATING EQUIPMENT —
SOLAR SYSTEMS

Corning Glass Works
Corning, NY 14830

Energy Systems, Inc.
941-D Anistad Ct.
El Cajon, CA 92020

Northrup, Inc.
302 Nichols Dr.
Hutchins, TX 75141

Raypak, Inc.
31111 Agoura Rd.
Westlake Village, CA 91361

Revere Copper and Brass, Inc.
P. O. Box 151
Rome, NY 13440

Reynolds Metal Co.
2315 Dominquez St.
Torrance, CA 90508

Solar Power Corp.
930 Clocktower Pkwy.
New Port Richey, FL 33552

Solar Ventures, Inc.
P. O. Box 1028
Baytown, TX 77520

Solarsystems, Inc.
1802 Dennis Dr.
Tyler, TX 75701

HYDROPONIC NUTRIENTS

Artex Hydroponics
Mena, AR 71953

Continental Nutriculture
P. O. Box 6751
Lubbock, TX 79413

Hydroculture, Inc.
P. O. Box 1655
Glendale, AZ 85301

Hydrofarms, Inc.
2405 T. O. Harris Rd.
Box 144-H
Mansfield, TX 76063

Hydro-Gardens, Inc.
P. O. Box 9707
Colorado Springs, CO 80932

Nutri-Sol Chemical Co., Inc.
4508 W. Osborne
P. O. Box 15124
Tampa, FL 33684

Robert B. Peters Co., Inc.
2833 Pennsylvania St.
Allentown, PA 18105

Dr. E. Saub
525 N. Colgate Ave.
Anaheim, CA 92801

2 J's and 1 D of Houston
7202 Brownwood
Houston, TX 77020

HYDROPONIC UNITS WITH CONTROLLED ENVIRONMENT

Commercial Units

Artex Hydroponics
Mena, AR 71953

Aquafarming Technology, Inc.
Hokum Rock Rd.
East Dennis, MA 02641

Creative Growing Systems, Inc.
5612 S. Rice Ave.
Houston, TX 77081

Global Green
2100 Clearwater Dr.
Oakbrook, IL 60521

Hydro Farms, Inc.
2405 T. O. Harris Blvd.
Box 144H
Mansfield, TX 76063

Hydroculture, Inc.
P. O. Box 1655
Glendale, AZ 85301

Nurstead Investments Ltd.
6307 Yonge Street
Toronto, Canada M2M3X7

Home Units

Aquaponics
22135 Ventura Blvd.
Woodland Hills, CA 91364

Aqua-Ponics of Anaheim
1040 E. Vermont Ave.
Anaheim, CA 92805

Aquafarming Technology, Inc.
Hokum Rock Rd.
East Dennis, MA 02641

Hydro-Con (Wick System)
11870 Beach Blvd.
Stanton, CA 90680

Specialty Gardens, Ltd.
90 Earlton Rd.
Agincourt, Ontario M1T 2R6
Canada

Waterworks Gardenhouse
P. O. Box 2599
Castro Valley, CA 94546

Indoor Units

Aquafarming Technology, Inc.
Hokum Rock Rd.
East Dennis, MA 02641

Aqua-Ponics of Anaheim
1040 E. Vermont Ave.
Anaheim, CA 92805

Dewey Compton Enterprises, Inc.
P. O. Box 2306
Houston, TX 77001

Hydro-Con (Wick System)
11870 Beach Blvd.
Stanton, CA 90680

Hydroponic Hobbies
302 Town & Country Village
Sunnyvale, CA 94086

Sturdi Products
5633 Richmond, Suite 204
Houston, TX 77057

Specialty Gardens, Ltd.
90 Earlton Rd.
Agincourt, Ontario M1T 2R6
Canada

MIST BLOWERS

Buffalo Turbine
Agricultural Equipment Co.
195 Industrial St.
Gowanda, NY 14070

H. D. Hudson Manufacturing
154 E. Erie St.
Chicago, IL 60611

Solo Industries, Inc.
Box 5030
Newport News, VA 23605

Vandermolen Corp.
Box 967
W. Caldwell, NJ 07006

Wolfe Wholesale Florist
Box 330
Waco, TX 76708

MIXES — PEAT TYPE

Annapolis Peat Moss Co.
Berwick, Nova Scotia
Canada

Dacus Supply Co.
2901 Montgomery
Fort Worth, TX 76107

Jiffy-Pot Co. of America
Box 338
W. Chicago, IL 60185

Keyes Fibre Co.
Box 806
New Iberia, LA 70560

W. R. Grace & Co.

Horticultural Products
62 Whittemore Ave.
Cambridge, Mass. 02140

Dallas, TX

*Most greenhouse supply
 companies*

PESTICIDES AND FUNGICIDES

May be found at most greenhouse
supply companies and local garden centers.

Fungicides

Botran
Tuco Products
Division of Upjohn Co.
Agricultural Chemical Division
Kalamazoo, MI 49001

Exotherm-Termil and Bravo
Diamond Shamrock Corp.
1100 Superior Ave.
Cleveland, OH 44114

Captan (Orthocide)
Chevron Chemical Co.
Ortho Division
200 Bush St.
San Francisco, CA 94210

Karathane
Tennessee Corp.
55 W. Marietta St., N.W.
Atlanta, GA 30303

Rohm & Haas Co.
Independence Mall West
Philadelphia, PA 19105

Kelthane
E. C. Geiger
Box 285
Harleysville, PA 19438

Maneb (Dithane M-22)
Rohm & Haas Co.
Independence Mall West
Philadelphia, PA 19105

Manzate
E. I. DuPont De Nemours & Co.
Wilmington, DE 19808

Terraclor
Agricultural Division
Monsanto Co.
800 North Lindberg Blvd.
St. Louis, MO 63166

Pesticides

**Smokes: Vapona (DDVP),
   Lindane, Aphid**
Smoke, Thiodan

Fuller Co. (Fulex)
226 Washington St.
Wovern, MA 01801

Thiodan Smoke
Black Leaf Products Co.
667 N. State St.
Elgin, IL 60612

*Other Pesticide, Fungicide and
Fumigant Supliers*

B & G Co.
2419 South Blvd.
Houston, TX 77006

Big State Chemical
2822 Leeland
Houston, TX 77003

Brighton By-Products Co., Inc.
P. O. Box 23
New Brighton, PA 15066

E. C. Geiger
Box 285
Harleysville, PA 19438

Whitmire Laboratories
   (Resmethrin)
3568 Tree Court Industrial Blvd.
St. Louis, MO 63122

Wolfe Wholesale Florist
Box 330
Waco, TX 76708

pH TESTERS

**Nitrazine Paper — most drug
   stores**

Analytical Measurements, Inc.
31 Willow St.
Chatham, NJ 07009

Aquaponics
22135 Ventura Blvd.
Woodland Hills, CA 91364

Aquality, Inc.
8939 Mason Ave.
Chatsworth, CA 91311

Beckman Instruments, Inc.
Cedar Grove, NJ 07009

Continental Nutriculture
P. O. Box 6751
Lubbock, TX 79413

132

Hydro-Con
11870 Beach Blvd.
Stanton, CA 90680

Scientific Products
1155 W. 23 St.
Tempe, AZ

Taylor Chemicals
7300 York Rd.
Baltimore, MD 21204

PLASTIC FILM (polyethylene, vinyl, and others)

Apopka Growers Supply, Inc.
P. O. Box Drawer K
Apopka, FL 32703

Chevron Chemical Corp.
200 Bush St.
San Francisco, CA 94120

DAO Corporation
P. O. Box 659
Terre Haute, IN 47808

Environmental Structures
7600 Wall St.
Cleveland, OH 44125

Ethyl Corporation
Visqueen Division
Box 2422
Baton Rouge, LA 70821

B. F. Goodrich Co.
500 S. Main St.
Akron, OH 44318

Goodyear Tire and Rubber Co.
Plastics Division
Akron, OH 44305

Growers International
6352 Alder St.
Houston, TX 77036

Monsanto Co.
200 N. Seventh St.
Kenilworth, NJ 07033

Monsanto 602
Monsanto Commercial Products
   Company
P. O. Box 503
Union, NJ 07083

Texas Greenhouse Co., Inc.
2717 St. Louis Ave.
Fort Worth, TX 76110

Union Carbide Corporation
Films Division
7633 W. 65 St.
Chicago, IL 61638

Uniroyal, Inc.
Chemical Division
Naugatuck, CT 06770

POLLINATORS

Artificial Fruit Set Sprays

Science Products Co., Inc.
5801 N. Tripp Ave.
Chicago, IL 60646

Vibrators

DAO Corporation
P. O. Box 659
Terre Haute, IN 47808

Jednak Floral Co.
Box 1917
Columbus, OH 43216

Plant Products Co., Ltd.
Port Credit, Ontario
Canada

PROPAGATING MATS

Famco
300 Lake Rd.
Medina, OH 44256

George J. Ball, Inc.
West Chicago, IL 60185

Many greenhouse suppliers

133

PUMPS

Beckett Co.
2521 Willowbrook Rd.
Dallas, TX 75220
or
Beckett Co.
Western Division
1420 Lawrence St.
Los Angeles, CA 90021

W. W. Grainger, Inc.
5959 W. Howard St.
Chicago, IL 60648
(Offices in most cities)

Little Giant Pump Co.
3810 N. Tulsa St.
Oklahoma City, OK 73112

Schenk & Associates
8415 Bluebonnet
Dallas, TX 75209

PROPORTIONERS

Young Industries
1033 Wright Avenue
Mountain View, CA 94043

ROOTING POWDER & MIXES

George J. Ball, Inc.
West Chicago, IL 60185

Many greenhouse suppliers, nursery and garden centers.

SEED SUPPLIERS

Cucumbers — European Seedless

George J. Ball, Inc.
West Chicago, IL 60185
or
George Ball Pacific, Inc.
Box 10175
Palo Alto, CA 94303

Herbst Bros., Inc.
1000 N. Main, Box 96
Brewster, NY 10501

Lakeshore Equipment & Supply
    Company
10237 Berea Rd.
Cleveland, OH 44102

Stokes Seeds
St. Catherines, Ontario L25 6R6
Canada

Lettuce — Greenhouse Varieties

George J. Ball, Inc.
West Chicago, IL 60185
or
George Ball Pacific, Inc.
Box 10175
Palo Alto, CA 94303
(Bibb, Grand Rapids, Butterhead,
    Buttercrunch)

Burgess Plant and Seed Co.
Galesburg, MI 49053
(Bibb, Grand Rapids)

W. Atlee Burpee Co.
Clinton, IA 52732
(Bibb, Boston, Butter King,
    Grand Rapids)

Dessert Seed Co., Inc.
Box 181
El Centro, CA 92243
or
Dessert Seed Co.
Box 666
Nyssa, OR 97913
(Bibb, Butter King, Chessibb,
    Grand Rapids H-54)

Grand Rapids Seed Growers, Inc.
401 – 403 Ionia Ave., S.W.
Grand Rapids, MI 49502
(Bibb, Grand Rapids H-54)

Joseph Harris Co., Inc.
Moreton Farm
Rochester, NY 14624
(Bibb, Bibb Summer, Boston,

Chessib, Grand Rapids H-54, Waldman's Green)

Herbst Bros., Inc.
1000 N. Main St., Box 96
Brewster, N.Y. 10509
(Bibb, Summer Bibb,
  Grand Rapids)

Holmes Seed Co.
Box 9087, 2125 46 St., N.W.
Canton, OH 44709
(Bibb Summer, Boston, Grand
  Rapids H-54, Waldman's Green)

Keystone Seed Co.
Box 1438
Hollister, CA 95023
(Boston, Chessibb, Grand
  Rapids H-54)

Letherman, Inc.
501 McKinley Ave., N.W.
Canton, OH 44702
(Bibb, Bibb Summer, Boston,
  Butter King, Grand Rapids,
  Waldman's Green)

Stokes Seeds, Inc.
Box 548
Buffalo, NY 14240
(Ostinata, Domineer, Butter
  King, Grand Rapids,
  Waldman's Green)

Otis S. Twilley
P. O. Box 230
Salisbury, MD 21801
(Butter King, Grand Rapids)

Vaughns Seed Co.
5300 Katrine Ave.
Downers Grove, IL 60515
(Bibb, Boston, Butter King,
  Grand Rapids)

Tomatoes—Greenhouse Varieties

All of the tomato varieties and hybrids listed are good and are the most widely used in greenhouse culture. I have had better yields using such varieties as Tropic, Manapal, and Floradel in the more temperate climates of the United States. Many of the other hybrids and varieties are possibly more suitable for northern areas. Market demand varies as to size, color, and flavor of the tomatoes.

The suppliers listed have the indicated varieties and hybrids available. Other seed companies may also have one or more of those listed.

George J. Ball, Inc.
West Chicago, IL 60185
or
George Ball Pacific, Inc.
Box 10175
Palo Alto, CA 94303
(Tropic, Floradel, Manapal, Tuck-
  cross Hybrids, Michigan-Ohio
  Hybrids, Ohio-Indiana Hybrids,
  Ohio WR-7)

Eureka Greenhouses
6894 Lafayette Rd.
Greenville, MI 48838
(Michigan-Ohio WR-7, Ohio-
  Indiana, Michigan 138,
  Michigan-Ohio WR-3)

Gortsema Greenhouses
5940 Clyde Park Ave., S.W.
Grand Rapids, MI 49509
(Michigan-Ohio WR-7, Michigan-
  Ohio)

Holwerda Greenhouses
612 28 St. S.E.
Grand Rapids, MI 48508
(Wolverine 119)

Porter and Son, Seedsmen
Box 104
Stephenville, TX 76401
(Tropic, Floradel, Manapal,
  Tuckcross Hybrids)

Stokes Seeds, Inc.
Box 548
Buffalo, NY 14240
(Vendor, Tuckcross Hybrids,
  Michigan-Ohio WR-7, Michigan-
  Ohio, Michigan 138, Vantage,
  Vinequeen, Ohio WR-7, Ohio
  WR-25)

The following suppliers offer many varieties of vegetable seeds. Some may have one or more of the above named varieties of cucumber, lettuce, and tomato. Most of the preceding suppliers carry extensive lines of other vegetable seeds.

Brawley Seed Co., Inc.
Mooresville, NC 28115

W. Atlee Burpee Co.
P. O. Box 6929
Philadelphia, PA 19432

Joseph Harris Co., Inc.
75 Moreton Farm
Rochester, NY 14624

The Vaughn Jacklin Corporation
5300 Katrine Ave.
Downers Grove, IL 60515

Leonard and Son
Piqua, OH 45356

Letherman, Inc.
501 McKinly Ave., N.W.
Canton, OH 44702

Mellingers Nursery
North Lima, OH 44452

Northrup, King and Co.
P. O. Box 7746
Boise, ID 83707
(Offices in many cities)

Pan-American Seed Co.
Box 438
West Chicago, IL 60185

George W. Park Seed Co.
530 Cokesbury Rd.
Greenwood, SC 29647

P. H. Shumway
Rockford, IL 61101

SEEDLINGS — TOMATO AND OTHERS

Artex Hydroponics
Mena, AR 71953

Famco
300 Lake Rd.
Medina, OH 44256

Hydro Farms, Inc.
2405 T. O. Harris Rd.
Box 144-H
Mansfield, TX 76063

Omaha Plant Farms
P. O. Box 787 AV
Omaha, TX 75571

Speedlings, Inc.
P. O. Box 7098
Sun City, FL 33586

SHADE CLOTH

Paramount Perlite Co.
Paramount, CA 90723

Shade Corporation of America
500 Clarksville St.
Cornelia, GA 30531

SHADING COMPOUNDS

The Garland Co.
3800 E. 91 St.
Cleveland, OH 44105

Texas Greenhouse Co., Inc.
2717 St. Louis Ave.
Fort Worth, TX 76110

Wolfe Wholesale Florist
Box 330
Waco, TX 76708

SUN CLEAR

Solar Sunstill, Inc.
Selauket, NY 11733

TEST KITS — TISSUE TESTING, SOIL TESTING

Continental Nutriculture
P. O. Box 6751
Lubbock, TX 79413

The Edwards Laboratory
P. O. Box 318
Norwalk, OH 44857
(Spurway)

E. C. Geiger Co.
P. O. Box 285
Harleysville, PA 19438

LaMotte Chemical Products Co.
Chestertown, MD 21620

Soil Testing Laboratory
Purdue University
Agronomy Dept.
Lafayette, IN 47907

Sudbury Laboratory, Inc.
Box 1302
Sudbury, MA 01776

Van Walter & Rogers Scientific
P. O. Box 3200
San Francisco, CA 94119
(Offices in most major cities)

THERMOMETERS — MAXIMUM-MINIMUM

Ward Brook
Box 99
East Candia, NH 03040

Taylor Instruments
4930 Cranswick
Houston, TX 77041
(Offices in most major cities)

THERMOSTATS AND HUMIDISTATS

W. W. Grainger, Inc.
5959 W. Howard St.
Chicago, IL 60648
(Offices in most major cities)

Penn Controls, Inc.
1302 E. Monroe
Goshen, IN 46526

Texas Greenhouse Co., Inc.
2717 St. Louis Ave.
Fort Worth, TX 76110
Local electrical supply houses

TWINE — POLY

Famco
300 Lake Rd.
Medina, OH 44256

J. E. Fricke Co.
40 N. Front St.
Philadelphia, PA 19106

TIMERS

W. W. Grainger, Inc.
5959 W. Howard St.
Chicago, IL 60648
(Offices most major cities)

Paragon Electric Co., Inc.
1600 Twelfth St.
Two Rivers, WI 54241

VERMICULITE

Dacus Supply Co.
2901 Montgomery
Fort Worth, TX 76107

Texas Vermiculite Co.
Box 6306
Dallas, TX 75222

VINE CLIPS — PLASTIC

Famco
300 Lake Rd.
Medina, OH 44256

Hansen Manufacturing Co.
2050 Sunnydale Blvd.
Clearwater, FL 33518

WATERING SYSTEMS

George J. Ball, Inc.
West Chicago, IL 60185
or
George Ball Pacific, Inc.
Box 10175
Palo Alto, CA 94303

The Cameron Co., Inc.
108 Runyon Ave.
Deal, NJ 07723

Chapin Watermatics, Inc.
368 N. Colorado Ave.
Watertown, NY 13601

Ickes-Braun Glasshouses
Box 147
Deerfield, IL 60015

Jednak Floral Co.
Box 1917
Columbus, OH 43216

Index

140

Afterword

Throughout this book I have used the male term when referring to hydroponic growers. This is a mistake common to most male writers. Some of the best crops I have ever seen were grown by ladies and I have known a great many women who have bought and operated their own units, and almost without exception they have been successful. So to all of the ladies who are both present and future hydroponic growers, my apologies and best wishes.